2011.

To Linz & Eugene,

BRITAIN
Goes Camping

happy camping!
and happy christmas,
lots of love from
Jan, Paulo Joy
xx
x

CAMPING, COOKING AND EXPLORING
THE GREAT OUTDOORS

DON PHILPOTT

National Trust

First published in the United Kingdom in 2011 by
National Trust Books
10 Southcombe Street
London W14 0RA

An imprint of Anova Books Ltd

ISBN: 9781907892073

A CIP catalogue record for this book is available from
the British Library.

20 19 18 17 16 15 14 13 12 11
10 9 8 7 6 5 4 3 2 1

Printed by 1010 Printing International Ltd, China
Reproduction by Mission Productions, Hong Kong

This book can be ordered direct from the publisher at
the website: www.anovabooks.com, or try your local
bookshop. Also available at National Trust shops,
including www.nationaltrustbooks.co.uk.

MIX
Paper from
responsible sources
FSC® C016973

CONTENTS

INTRODUCTION

Camping is fun. It is affordable and can be tailored to suit almost all needs. Whether you set off on foot, on your bicycle or pack up all your gear in the car and drive to a campsite, you can spend a fun weekend relaxing with family and friends or several weeks exploring the many wonders the countryside has to offer.

For a lot less than the cost of a week's accommodation at a decent hotel, you can buy everything you need for a family camping holiday – and you can use the equipment again and again for years to come. The chances are that if you have the gear you will enjoy a lot more spontaneous mini-breaks as well. The weekend is coming up, the weather forecast is great so simply throw the tent, sleeping bags and cooking equipment in the car and head off.

There is no shortage of places to go with more than 4,000 campsites in the UK and an enormous range of things to do when you get there. You can laze on a beach, walk in the countryside or camp on a farm and even help out with the chores if you wish. For those who want to be more active, you can stay near an activity centre and go rock climbing, learn outdoor skills, visit a historic house or garden, or whatever else takes your fancy. Camping gives you the freedom to roam, to commune with nature and have a really great time.

Camping is no longer seen as 'roughing it' because of the advances in equipment. There are now portable flush loos and shower tents, camping fridges, sophisticated gas stoves, portable TVs and so on. Tents are light, easy to erect and spacious, and camping sites have improved almost beyond recognition to compete with other holiday

left: One of the great pleasures of camping is being able to enjoy spectacular scenery as you look out of your tent. This fabulous view is from the National Trust campsite at Wasdale Head, Cumbria.

above: Camping has changed dramatically in the last few decades, as has the equipment available to us. This picture was taken the 1950s at St. Brelade's, Jersey, considered by many to be the most beautiful of all the Channel Island bays. While camping has changed, it is still as much fun as ever.

choices. Many offer a wide range of facilities including amusements, restaurants and shops.

Camping is not just affordable; it is a great way to meet new friends. Most campers are by their very nature social creatures and it doesn't take long for the circle around an inviting campfire to grow as new friends are made.

You may have a favourite destination that you and your family keep going back to or you might like to explore – you are never likely to run out of locations. You can camp in the hills or close to the beach, near forests or a beautiful lake teeming with fish. You can camp year round if you want to and there are always things to do and new places to see. The only real downside to camping is the unpredictable weather but even that is less of a challenge than it used to be. Equipment and outdoor clothing is so good today that you are protected from all but the worst elements. As the rain pours down outside, you can, if you want, sit in your tent watching a programme on your portable, battery-operated TV although I think it is more fun to play games, especially if you are a family with children. Fun is an important element of camping as well. Getting out and walking is healthy and if you have children, there are many ways you can make their experience even more enjoyable with games and fun projects, several of which are described later in this book (see from page 138).

I've been camping for more than 50 years and have had the good fortune to pitch tents in many countries around the world with family and friends. While some of these countries offered spectacular scenery, very few provided the enormous diversity that you can find in the UK. There are the rugged cliffs and

below: There are few sights more beautiful than a shaded woodland carpeted with bluebells. This picture was taken in the woods to the west of the house at National Trust's Speke Hall, Merseyside, although similar scenes can be found all over the country if you get out and explore.

quaint villages of the South West;
the glorious scenery of Northern
Ireland; the magnificent beaches
and mountains of Wales; the marshes,
beaches and birdlife of East Anglia,
and everything in between.

Apart from being able to explore
all these wonderful places and discover
their rich histories and architectural
splendours, there is the countryside itself
to explore. It doesn't matter how old you
are, there is always something new to
learn about nature.

My favourite way to enjoy the
countryside is on foot following
ancient paths or heading up into the
hills. You see so much more of nature
this way, and by stopping and
observing you will learn more – something you can't do if you are speeding past
in a car. Apart from the scenery and wildlife there is so much else to see. You can
marvel at centuries-old stone walls, explore remnants of industrial archeology
and discover tucked-away villages far off the beaten track.

above: We miss so much tearing around the
countryside in our cars, especially our glorious
wildlife, like this rabbit eating its fill of buttercups
and thistles in a Shropshire field.

The more effort you put in to something, the more you will get out of it. So
the better able you are to identify the birds, trees, flowers and animal tracks that
you see, the more you will enjoy your visits to the countryside. If you can pass on
this information to your children, it will encourage them too to take a greater
interest in learning more about their environment and, hopefully, take steps to
protect and preserve it. That, of course, means following the Countryside Code,
which can be paraphrased as Respect, Protect and Enjoy. That way we can all
enjoy the countryside – and camping in it – for generations to come.

A LITTLE HISTORY...

The British have been walking in the countryside for both leisure and health for over 200 years. It was London doctor A.F.N. Willich who wrote in 1799 that walking was 'the most rational means of preserving health and prolonging life'. Regular and daily walking 'cannot be too much recommended to the citizen, who in the present age is so much harassed with nervous and hypochondriacal complaints,' he said. Little, it seems, has changed.

Two or three centuries ago walking was often the only way to get around for most people although few ventured further than the next village. There is an account, however, of Foster Powell who, in 1773, walked from London to York and back, averaging 72 miles (116km) a day. In the next century Leslie Stephen, a Cambridge academic, was noted for his long-distance walking. One day he walked 50 miles (80km) from Cambridge to London to attend a dinner at the Alpine Club. In 1879 he started the Sunday Tramps, a club whose members met every Sunday to walk in the countryside around London.

In the 19th century walking for pleasure became fashionable and special walks were created to allow city folks access to the countryside, especially in and around spa towns such as Bath, Cheltenham and Tunbridge Wells. Towards the end of the 19th century hotels opened in the Lake District catering to the summer walkers. Beatrice Webb wrote about her 'long rambling walks in this lovely country' around Lake Windermere in 1879.

In 1879 Robert Louis Stevenson published *Travels with a Donkey in the Cévennes*. It is one of the great walking memoirs of all time. He was following a long literary tradition – William Wordsworth wrote about his walking tour on the Continent in 1790 and of his later ramblings in the Lake District, which also inspired some of his greatest poetry. John Keats wrote of his more arduous walk in Scotland and of his elation – and relief – at scaling Ben Nevis.

left: *Hiker and Camper* magazine, June 1931.

above: Hike for Health poster for Southern Railway, 1932, showing a couple striding happily along in the countryside. Affordable transport encouraged the masses to get out of cities and into the countryside.

Stevenson's travels through central France in 1878 were a little eccentric. He didn't take a tent but had a large sleeping sack stuffed with some books, a leg of cold mutton, a bottle of wine, an egg-beater and lots of bread. The weight was so great that he then had to buy Modestine, a donkey, to carry it all. That walk inspired a love of travel that continued until Stevenson's death in 1894 and while today he is remembered for books such as *Kidnapped, Treasure Island* and *Dr Jekyll and Mr Hyde*, his writings about his travels in Britain, North America and the South Pacific are still inspiring.

While the British have been ramblers and walkers for more than 200 years, camping is a relatively new pastime. The first campers are believed to have been six gentlemen wearing tweeds and starched collars. They pitched heavy canvas tents in an orchard in Wantage, Oxfordshire in 1901 and boiled water for their tea on a roaring camp fire.

below: Looking towards the fells from the spectacular National Trust campsite at Wasdale Head in the Lake District. Today's tents are roomier, lighter and certainly more colourful.

One member of that group was Thomas Hiram Holding, a tailor, who produced the first lightweight, portable tent. He formed the Association of Cycle Campers, which by 1906 had several hundred members. He also wrote *The Camper's Handbook,* since, as the pastime was so new, many of its participants needed all the advice they could get. Camping remained the preserve of 'gentlemen' until the end of the First World War when its popularity mushroomed as it was affordable to the masses. In fact, it became so popular in the 1930s that many farmers were setting aside fields as campsites. In return, local authorities passed bylaws preventing the erection of 'moveable dwellings', namely tents. In 1936 the Public Health Act banned the sale of bread, butter and milk on campsites, which were limited to one tent an acre.

By then, however, camping was so popular that there was even an official Camping Club. It fought many of the restrictions and got them lifted from officially registered campsites.

After the Second World War and especially in the early 1950s, new materials such as nylon were used to make lightweight tents and camping re-emerged as the most popular holiday for the masses. For many it provided the only affordable opportunity to holiday. Today there are more than 4,000 campsites throughout the UK – more than enough for a lifetime's vacations.

DID YOU KNOW?

Camping has remained popular over the decades although equipment and materials have changed beyond recognition in the last 50 years. A family-sized canvas tent weighed 15kg (33lb) in 1945; today four-person tents weighing in at less than 2kg (4½lb) are commonplace.

In 1935, sleeping bags had not been invented, and most campers used a canvas camp bed with blankets and sheets. The legs of the camp bed would be stood in upturned jam jars to stop earwigs crawling up! Bedrolls, introduced in the 1940s and 50s, weighed up to 10kg (22lb). Today a lightweight sleeping bag weighs around 1kg (2¼lb) and costs from around £10, while a top-of-the-range four-season bag for serious campers can cost over £400.

SECTION ONE:

CAMPING KNOW-HOW

PRACTICAL INFORMATION

Camping is fun but it is not just a question of buying a tent, a couple of sleeping bags and a camping stove and rushing off to spend a night out. It will be much more fun if you plan your purchases wisely so that you have the right equipment for your purposes and it is capable of protecting you from the sort of weather you are likely to face.

If you are a family camper and everything goes into the back of the car, you can choose a much more spacious, heavier tent and take with you a lot more equipment to make your stay more comfortable. If you do encounter really bad weather, you can either sit it out in the tent or pack up and head home.

below: When you are looking for a good site always make sure that it is OK to camp there. There are usually signs to help you.

There are a few other important dos and don'ts as well. The most important thing is to remember and abide by the Countryside Code (see page 18). Next, respect the privacy of others. Most campers are sociable but some want their peace and quiet so show consideration around the campsite, don't make undue noise – especially late in the evening – and keep your campsite clean. For example, don't pour the tasty fat from your breakfast frying pan on to the grass, where it might attract swarms of insects, such as wasps, to feed on it.

If you have a dog, keep it on a lead around the campsite and try not to let it yap; make sure it has water and shade; and, finally, exercise it away from the camping area. As with any public area, you should also take care to pick up after your dog and dispose of the waste properly.

above: It's great to take the family pet with you on camping trips but always keep dogs on a leash around the campsite – for their safety and the safety of others.

Keep noise to a minimum, especially if you have a radio, music player or TV. Children's games can be boisterous; make sure they keep the noise down and do not let your kids play ball where tents become goals. Warn them about guy lines, tent pegs and other potential hazards. If everyone considers their neighbours, you will all have a great time.

The best way to be a good camper and neighbour is to know and follow the campground's regulations. Read the rules when you arrive and make sure all the members of your group understand them. Always respect other people's space. When you leave, make sure you take all your belongings – including stray tent pegs – with you and dispose of your rubbish properly. Leave the site as you would like to find it.

REMEMBER THE COUNTRYSIDE CODE

There is a great need in modern times to reconnect our lives to the landscape. This has to start with an understanding of the land. The National Trust works hard to do this, encouraging people to connect with the land but also to conserve and appreciate it. People are asked to abide by the Countryside Code when enjoying the land around them. Scotland has its own Outdoor Access Code, as does Northern Ireland. Particular areas and some National Trust properties have separate bylaws that may restrict a small number of activities.

1 **Shut gates after you.** Using gates and stiles is highly recommended and is easier than clambering over walls, which can damage hedges and fences. Shutting gates after use also prevents any livestock escaping.

2 **Keep dogs under control.** Even the best-behaved and best-loved dogs will be seen as predators by the rest of the natural world. Dogs and dog walkers are welcome at National Trust coast and countryside sites, but there are occasions when a small number of dog owners cause problems for other visitors and vulnerable wildlife. To avoid distressing livestock or wildlife keep dogs on leads and under close control at all times. Particularly observe local notices on the need to keep dogs on a lead at sensitive times of the year, such as during the breeding season for ground-nesting birds, when sheep are lambing or deer are having calves. You may also need to abide by seasonal access restrictions on popular beaches in the summer. Where access for dogs has been restricted, the Trust attempts to find suitable alternative

left: Exploring the countryside with the family dog – like this couple on the National Trust's Castle Drogo estate, in Devon – adds to your enjoyment provided the animal is always properly controlled.

above: If you have to open a gate while you are out walking, always close it behind you.

locations to walk a dog nearby. Please also bear in mind that dogs should not be left in cars on hot days and dog mess should be taken away with you.

3   **Keep to paths.** By keeping to paths, you not only avoid trampling and disturbing many habitats but you can also move quietly and quickly, and in doing so enhance your chances of seeing wildlife.

4   **Do not pick flowers.** To help maintain the beautiful plant life, try to enjoy flowers in their habitat and leave them where they are so they can flourish and grow. Use a notebook or a digital camera to capture specimens for later identification back at home.

5   **Take all litter home.** That means everything, including apple cores and banana peels. Take pride in leaving the place exactly as you found it.

6   **Be careful with fire.** Any unguarded naked flame from matches, cigarettes and barbecues is capable of untold damage if the conditions are right. Forest or grassland fires can be disastrous for many lives, both wild and human. Check local bylaws and campsite policy to ensure that lighting fires is allowed in and around your campsite area.

7   **Be careful on the roads.** In the countryside the roads become narrower and more winding and therefore more dangerous. So be aware of this if you are walking or driving on them.

CHOOSING THE RIGHT EQUIPMENT

TENTS

The great thing about the British weather is that it is so unpredictable. The West Country had its hottest June on record in 2010 while November 2009 was the wettest month ever recorded in the UK. So when buying a tent always plan for the worst weather imaginable.

Over the last few years tent designs have improved enormously; the materials are stronger, lighter and more weatherproof and most can be put up very quickly. They also come in an enormous range of shapes and sizes from teepees to A-frames, hoops, domes and freestanding to the aptly named cabin tents, which have multiple rooms and windows.

A-frame is the traditional tent style with two upright poles, one at each end. Sometimes a third pole is used in the centre to form a ridge. They have steep sides and offer little head room, which is why other, more modern styles are now widely preferred.

Cabin tents are enormous and designed for use with car camping or other forms of camping where weight is not an issue. They are heavy and large, but offer an enormous amount of internal space. They usually consist of a number of poles jointed together for easy assembly, and form a pentagonal structure with a high ceiling and more than sufficient floor space.

Dome tents have a very simple structure and are available in a wide variety of sizes ranging from

left: Domes are now one of the most popular tents worldwide because they are light, roomy and easy to put up.

right: Relaxing at the National Trust campsite at Wasdale Head, Cumbria.

lightweight two-person tents with limited headroom up to six- or nine-person tents with headroom exceeding 180cm (6ft). These may be single wall, or single wall with partial flysheet, or double wall. Depending on the pole arrangement, some models pitch outer tent first, while others pitch inner tent first. The former helps keep the inner tent dry, but the latter is easier to pitch. The basic dome has a rectangular floor and two poles that cross at the peak; each pole runs in a curve from one bottom corner, up to the peak, and then down to the diagonally opposite bottom corner. There are usually special fittings at each corner, which fit into sockets at the ends of each pole – pole tension keeps everything in shape. The poles can run on either the inside or outside of the tent fabric. When located on the interior, poles are held in place by a variety of means including hook-and-loop style straps, clips and other fastening hardware. Poles that are located on the outside of the tent fabric are attached via fabric pole sleeves or plastic clips. Dome tents do not require guy ropes and pegs for structural integrity as they are considered freestanding, but must be pegged down in high winds.

Tunnel tents offer more usable internal space than a dome tent with the same ground area, but almost always need guy ropes and pegs to stay upright. These are usually double-wall tents. Sizes range from one-person tents with very limited headroom up to eight- or ten-person tents with headroom exceeding 180cm (6ft). Tunnel tents have a low end profile making them great for high-wind situations. A basic tunnel tent uses three flexible poles, arranged as three parallel hoops, with tent fabric attached to form a tunnel. Smaller designs may use only two poles and larger designs may use four poles; the latter may have a sleeping area at each end and a living area in the middle.

Hybrid dome/tunnel tents are now common. One variation is to use a basic dome as the sleeping area; one or two hooped poles to one side are linked by a tunnel to the dome to provide a porch. Another variation is to use a large dome as the living area, with up to four tunnel extensions to provide sleeping areas.

Geodesic tents are essentially dome tents with two or more extra poles that crisscross the usual two poles to help support the basic shape and minimise the amount of unsupported fabric. This makes them more suitable

right: Family tents, like this one at Wasdale Head in Cumbria, give you spacious living and sleeping accommodation and almost all the comforts of home.

for use in snowy conditions and in strong winds. To help withstand strong winds they are rarely more than 120–150cm (4–5ft) high.

Single-hoop tents use just one flexible pole and are often sold as lightweight one- or two-person tents. These are the modern equivalent of older-style pup tents (the traditional inverted V-shaped tent with poles at either end), and have the same feature of somewhat limited headroom. Different styles may have the pole going either along or across the tent.

The pop-up tent has built-in very flexible hoops so that when unpacked, it springs into shape immediately, and so is extremely easy to set up. They are usually single skinned and only suitable for fair-weather camping. They should not be used in windy conditions.

For family camping, you really want a tent that everyone can stand up in and that has a thick, waterproof floor. Many tents now come with a 'bathtub' floor, which means the floor and lower walls combine to form a seamless perimeter that you

above: Tent designs have come a long way since this scene in 1910. This large family tent with spacious awning probably needed a horse and cart to transport it!

step over to get in and out. This prevents any water seeping into the tent. It has the added advantage of keeping out crawling insects.

The first decision you have to make when choosing a tent is what you are going to use it for, and the second decision is when you are going to use it.

Family camping

A family tent has to be spacious enough to accommodate all the family and its gear – and still afford some privacy if you are all sleeping together. Bigger is generally better – especially if you all have to hunker down inside during a summer daytime downpour.

Tents also have to have adequate ventilation or use breathable fabrics to prevent condensation build-up.

Many large family tents now come with built-in 'rooms' or zip-in dividers to create separate sleeping areas. Alternatively, you can have two tents – a larger one for the parents and rainy-day activities and the other for the children – although if you are using a camping site this will cost you extra. Some campsites also insist that people using very large family tents also pay for a double site because they take up so much room.

Choose a tent that can be erected easily. Most tents are not difficult to put up but some can be and the last thing you want to be doing in a downpour is still struggling to erect a tent when you should be inside it in the dry. Apart from the instructions that should come with the tent, many tent manufacturers have videos on their websites showing how to pitch it.

Flysheets are an essential extra if not already built into the design. Apart from being waterproof they should also be fire retardant. Awnings for larger tents are also good as they provide additional covered space and a shady place to sit if it is very hot.

A good tent should last several years if looked after properly so it is well worth spending a little more for quality.

Colour is also important – lighter coloured tents are cooler in the summer while darker coloured tents are a better choice for winter camping because they absorb solar energy.

Backpackers' tents

If you are backpacking, you need a tent that is light and compact without being claustrophobic. The sort of tent you buy will depend on when you are going to use it and how many people are going to sleep in it. Backpacking tents can usually sleep between one and three people and, obviously, the more people it accommodates the heavier it will be to carry, but the extra weight can be shared between you all.

Hoop tents are ideal for backpackers (see page 24). They resemble a tunnel tapering from front to back. They can be erected quickly and because of their low end profile can withstand gale-force winds. There is usually enough room to be able to sit up at the entrance.

below: Touring with tents grew in popularity in the 1930s as motorcars became affordable and people began to explore the great outdoors, both across Britain and further afield.

Putting up your tent

Having bought it, you have to be able erect it easily – so you need to practise. Take it out into the back garden and put the tent up a few times until you are totally familiar with it. If you have a pet dog, keep it on a leash while you put the tent up to avoid it scratching or tearing the fabric.

Keep the tent up overnight and sleep in it to see what it feels like – make this a special family adventure – and use the garden hose to make sure it is waterproof – better to find out this way than when camping in the countryside.

There are few things worse than sitting in your tent during a torrential

above: Most modern tents can be erected by one person although it is certainly easier – and faster – with two. Even if you are using a freestanding tent, it is a good idea to use pegs for added security.

downpour and watching a small tear appear and then grow steadily larger as the water starts to flood in. That is why you always need to check your equipment before going on a trip. You check the tent to make sure there is no mould in case it was put away slightly damp. You check to make sure there are no tears or anything else that might cause problems later on and you make sure that you have all the parts – poles, flysheets, guy ropes and so on – and that everything is in working order.

One thing people often skimp on is tent pegs – this is a big mistake. A lot of tents today don't need tent pegs or stakes. However, you should always have some pegs in case you need to secure the tent with extra guy ropes if a storm is coming. Plastic pegs will grip the ground, assuming you can hammer them home. If you are camping in a rocky area the chances are that the plastic pegs will crack or bend. Use lightweight titanium pegs that are very strong and can be hammered into all but the toughest ground. Always hammer tent pegs in at an angle for maximum strength rather than straight down.

When you return from your trip, spread the tent out until you are sure that it is completely dry and aired. Before storing, check seams for loose stitching and repair if necessary and apply a thin coating of silicon lubricant to the zippers.

SLEEPING BAGS AND MATS

There is nothing worse than a bad night's sleep in a tent – whatever the reason. The night seems to drag on forever and even if you do doze off, you wake up tired and unrested. The aim when camping is to make your bed away from home as comfortable as possible so that you nod off easily and have a great night's sleep. You can buy inflatable airbeds and luxury camp cots if you want to do it in style but most of us make do with sleeping bags and some sort of mat to go under them. The mat gives a little extra padding and helps insulate against any cold or damp from the ground.

A sleeping bag was traditionally a square blanket folded over and zipped on one or two sides. Today, sleeping bags come in all shapes and sizes but rectangular ones with a zip all down one side and across the bottom are best for family camping – and usually the cheapest (see below). You can sleep inside the bag if the night is chilly or fully unzip the sleeping bag and use it as a duvet. Choose sleeping bags stuffed with quality synthetic materials. They provide warmth and dry quickly if they get wet. Down and feather stuffing provides a lot of warmth but it is expensive and next to useless if it gets wet. Of course, if the sleeping bag has a waterproof shell, you can have whatever filling you prefer.

Like tents, backpacking sleeping bags get a 'seasons' rating. Sleeping-bag materials have improved so much in the last few years that whatever the rating, outer shells are usually waterproof and windproof while the insulation filling is light yet effective. Mummy-shaped bags taper from head to foot and contour to your body, helping to prevent loss of body heat but many people find them too constricting.

Choose a bag that you are going to be comfortable sleeping in. Full-length zips can let out heat but help you get into the bag more easily.

left: Sleeping bags come in all shapes and sizes but the most important thing when choosing one is that it must be comfortable and it must keep you warm whatever the weather conditions outside.

above: Taking your favourite pillow on a camping trip will help ensure a good night's sleep – much more comfortable than making do with a lumpy backpack or folded jeans!

Because they are bulky items, it is best to pack each sleeping bag into a stuff sack or compression sack, which allows all the air to be squeezed out so that it fits into a much smaller space.

Note: Most good sleeping bags will carry a European Standard Rating – EN 13537. This is a temperature rating that indicates the upper and lower limits at which the bag should be used, as well as the comfort measure and extreme measure. The ratings do not mean that the bag cannot be used when the temperature exceeds the upper and lower limits but it is a good indicator of how effective the bag will be. For instance the lower limit is defined as 'the temperature at which a standard man can sleep for eight hours in a curled position without waking', while the 'extreme' limit is 'the minimum temperature at which a standard woman can remain for six hours without risk of death from hypothermia (although frostbite is possible)'. Obviously it is not a good idea to use a particular sleeping bag anywhere near its extreme limit. Don't skimp on sleeping mats either. They should be thick enough to provide adequate insulation and support, as well as long and wide enough to accommodate your whole body.

Many backpackers choose smaller mats because they are lighter and more convenient to pack, but if you are driving to a campsite, why suffer? Choose the bigger mats and be more comfortable. If you are backpacking, don't carry the rolled up mat underneath your pack – if it rains all day, you don't want to be sleeping on a sodden mat. Use it as a liner inside your rucksack and pack all your other gear inside it. Pillows are another essential item when camping. Rolling up your jeans and using them

above: It never pays to skimp on the cost of a good sleeping bag. The more expensive bags will generally be better quality, will keep you warmer and last longer.

as a pillow does not really work and, besides, many children – and quite a few grown-ups – cannot go to sleep unless they have their favourite pillow.

RUCKSACKS AND BACKPACKS

Your choice of backpack (also called a knapsack, rucksack, pack, packsack or Bergen) will depend on what you plan to do. If you are backpacking you will need a large-capacity pack to carry all your equipment, extra clothes, food and so on. These large packs have heavy padded hip belts that help support the load – as the hips are stronger than the shoulders – while the shoulder straps are used mainly to stabilise the pack.

If you are going family camping, you will still need a small backpack or daypack to carry waterproofs, lunch, basic first-aid kit and so on. In this case, a day bag will be fine. If global warming continues to give us sweltering summers, you can get a daypack with a built in bladder that holds water and has a hands-free delivery system involving a tube and bite-valve.

right: Always try on a backpack before buying it to make sure it is comfortable and large enough for your needs.

CHOOSING THE RIGHT PACK

Frameless packs are usually best for lighter loads, such as daypacks, although some models do have waist belts, padded backs and padded shoulder straps. Because they lack a frame that provides additional support, concern has been expressed that frameless packs with very heavy loads can cause back injuries.

External frames, usually made of aluminium or light-weight metal alloy, can support packs that weigh 20kg (44lb) and more. The advantages are that the frame provides both good weight distribution and creates a ventilation gap between the pack and the walker's back.

Internal frames were introduced in the late 1960s. The frame is shaped to fit into the contour of your back so that it is more stable when walking. These packs should have at least one large internal pocket for most of your gear and one or more other smaller, easily accessible pockets for things you may need to get to in a hurry – your waterproofs for instance. A large pack can have a capacity of 100 litres (6,000 cubic inches) – enough space to pack for many days out. The downside is that as the pack fits snugly against you there is no ventilation space and so your back can get very warm and sweaty. However, internal frames have largely replaced external frames among serious backpackers.

The bodypack resembles a backpack with a waistcoat. As well as the pack it has pockets in the front that can be loaded and most of the weight is carried on the hips. It is great for wildlife photographers who need to have quick access to equipment but it is not a serious contender for backpackers or campers.

Always try the pack on in the shop. Consider: does it feel right, do the shoulder straps offer enough padding, is it big enough for everything you need? It's always better to buy a pack that may be bigger than you need than to get one that is too small. Backpack materials are also important because they have to be tough enough to withstand rips and tears and sufficiently waterproof to keep out the rain. Some backpacks are now made with reflective materials so that you can be seen in the dark.

As an added precaution when backpacking, you can get a backpack rain cover if there is not one already included as part of the rucksack. Make sure you get the

below: Small packs – like the ones carried by these walkers ascending Scafell Pike in Wasdale – are great for day hikes when you need to carry essentials such as food, waterproofs, water and first aid kit.

right size for your pack. They are ultra-light but waterproof and contoured to fit snugly all around the pack with cord locks to hold them on securely.

STOVES AND COOKING UTENSILS

One of the lightest single burner stoves weighs just 76g (2.7oz) and one gas cartridge can last a week. It takes about two minutes to boil 500ml (just under a pint) of water, which is very fast.

The heaviest cooking utensil I have ever used when camping was a cast iron Dutch oven, which weighed in at 11.4kg (25lb) and was used to create some magnificent dishes. Obviously the Dutch oven is not a good idea for the backpacker but if you are loading everything into the back of the car, but it should be one of the items you consider taking for your camping kitchen (if you are allowed campfires) because of its versatility.

Camping stoves can range from single and double burners using propane or butane gas, petrol, kerosene or other fuels, to full BBQ grills. There are even one-burner stoves that allow you to burn several different types of fuels, including unleaded petrol, which is great if the local shop has run out of your preferred fuel. Look for backpacking stoves with radiant burners or heat exchangers, which greatly increase efficiency.

Whatever fuel you are using, make sure you know how long a canister or fuel bottle will last. Also, if you are backpacking, make sure the fuel is packed securely in your rucksack so that it can't contaminate other items, especially food.

Camping stoves are easy to use and function even in the worst weather conditions but never try to cook inside your tent. In an emergency, if the weather is really bad, you can cook in the entrance to the tent but always have a water bottle handy in case of a sudden flare up.

Most camping stoves come with a base, which gives greater stability. You should always make sure your stove is on level ground. The last thing you want is for your pot to topple off just as your meal is ready. As an added precaution I like to choose a large flat rock and use it as the base for my stove. If it is windy I try to build a windbreak to protect the stove. This not only prevents the stove from being blown out or, worse, blown over, it also allows it to burn more efficiently so you conserve fuel. You can always use your backpack as a windbreak.

Campfires are the most fun way to cook food but whether you can have one depends on the rules of the campsite and the weather conditions. An odd spark can quickly develop into a wildfire if everything is bone dry. How to build a campfire and make it safe is dealt with later on (see pages 66–67).

Whether you are cooking on a campfire or a portable stove, you need cooking utensils to go with it. For backpackers there are all sorts of lightweight cookware sets available. They usually consist of two or three pots that nest together for easy and compact packing. They can be made of aluminium, stainless steel or even titanium for the ultimate in lightness and strength. An aluminium pot holder, which clamps on to the side of the pot, is the best way to take pots off the flame and avoid burnt fingers. A plastic or aluminium plate, bowl, mug and knife, fork and spoon complete your basic cook set.

If you are camping as a family and planning to stay in the same place for several days you can have quite an elaborate camp kitchen and bring along all your favourite utensils. This is one of those cases where you really can have everything, including the kitchen sink.

above and left: Camping stoves and cooking equipment are now so light and versatile that you can cook a gourmet meal on the trail if you want to – although bangers and beans are still great!

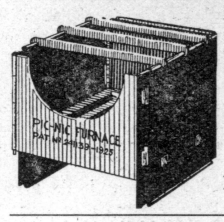

Invented and made by a Camper and is the handiest, safest, and most useful article yet invented for Picnic Parties of 12 or so, and Camps of 2 or 3 persons. Boils a 10-cup kettle in a few minutes. Burns wood or any solid fuel. When not in use, folds like a book to 6 in. by 1¼ in., and weighs only 2½ lb. Satisfaction guaranteed or money refunded.

MAVER'S "PICNIC" FURNACE

OPENS 6ins. SQUARE BY 6 ins. DEEP

Price
7/6

Postage 9*d*.

ARTHURLIE ENGINEERING CO.
BARRHEAD-BY-GLASGOW
SCOTLAND

above: Advertisement for Maver's Picnic Furnace, June, 1931, intended to cater for the masses who were just beginning to explore the countryside.

CLOTHES

The layer principle is best when you are camping. If it is very cold, wear several layers that can be peeled off as it gets warmer and vice versa. Lightweight man-made materials, such as polyester, are best as they dry so quickly – cotton may be natural but it dries slowly, and cotton socks will rub and can cause blisters when wet. The layer principle is not only to allow you to adapt to the temperature, it will also keep the body ventilated. There is no point in being protected from a piercing cold wind if your body is covered in sweat. Inner clothing layers should be able to wick moisture away from your body to keep you dry and outer layers should be waterproof and windproof. Jeans are great to wear outdoors but they are heavy and can take days to dry if they get really wet. Lightweight trousers and shorts are better as they dry very quickly; they are light and they don't take up much room.

Always wear clothing suitable to the terrain and the weather conditions you are likely to encounter. If you are planning to be out when it is likely to be cold always pack headgear and gloves. It's amazing how much body heat you lose from the top of your head in very cold weather.

FOOTWEAR

The right footwear is essential. Trainers and trail shoes are great for walking in most terrains as long as they provide grip and support. You don't want to be sliding around on wet grass or turning an ankle. If you are doing serious summer hill walking, lightweight boots are advisable as they do give you more grip and better ankle support. For hiking in the hills in the winter,

left: Choose the socks that are suitable for your needs. Hikers and backpackers need socks that will cushion the feet and stay dry.

move up a notch again and get some heavier duty boots. As a general rule when backpacking, the heavier your pack, the more support you need from your footwear.

Thanks to modern materials most outdoor footwear is breathable to prevent your feet from getting too hot and with waterproof liners to keep them dry. Sandals are fine around the campsite as they allow your feet to breathe after a day's walking.

Trainers and boots don't really need breaking in these days but it still makes sense to wear them for a few days before you leave for your camping trip to ensure they are not going to cause any problems.

above: Hiking boots and sturdy walking shoes will protect your feet and prevent slips on long hikes – but it's a good idea to air them out once you are back at the campsite.

Socks are also important. For serious walking look for socks with cushioning in the ball and heel to help reduce blisters, and choose materials that wick moisture away from the skin to keep the feet dry.

Always check your footwear before setting off on a trip. If the sole or heel of a boot is damaged, take another pair as the last thing you want is for your boots to start disintegrating when you are miles from anywhere.

CHOOSING FOOTWEAR

Don't be stingy when it comes to buying footwear. There's no point in trying to save a few pounds if the boots or trainers you buy are going to fall to pieces after a short time or fit so badly they'll give you blisters. When buying footwear, shop in the late afternoon when your feet are usually slightly swollen from being on them all day. The boot or trainer should fit snugly but not be tight and there should be some wriggle room for your toes, which should not be pressed up against the front of the footwear.

PLANNING A TRIP

The secret to any successful trip is the planning – knowing where to go, when to go, what to expect, what to do, what to take, and how to get there and back safely. If you plan on staying at a popular campsite it is best to make a reservation as far ahead as possible – and then ring to confirm it about four weeks prior to your arrival date.

If you have not visited this campsite before, do your homework before you go. Find out all you can about the area: places that you should make a point of visiting – historic homes, beautiful gardens, museums, attractions and so on – plus opening times and directions. Make the planning a family activity so that everyone can pick something they really want to do. Check the local tourist board's website. There may be additional information and special offers on tickets. Check out the National Trust's website to see which properties or open countryside it has nearby and, while you're at it, download one of their many walking or cycling routes to explore during your visit.

Without being too rigid, it is a good idea to plan your activities so that you know what you are going to be doing on most days. Build into your schedule one or two rest days for hanging out near the pool, on the beach or for shopping, and be flexible enough to take into account any changes caused by bad weather.

Another thing that needs careful planning is what you are going to eat. You should have a draft menu worked out for each day so that you know what ingredients you need to take with you and what you can buy locally. Menu planning is even more important if you are backpacking and not easily able to get to local stores or farm shops.

Backpackers also need to plan their journeys well and study the route they will take so they have a reasonably good idea of how much distance they can cover daily, what they want to see along the way as side trips and when they can expect to finish. You need to study the terrain because that will determine how far you can walk each day, and find out about the likely weather conditions to be encountered so that you can pack accordingly. If travelling with a group, try to calculate your average daily walking distances based on the slowest walker not the fastest. Never overestimate your ability. Don't work out a route that involves endless hours of hard walking over difficult terrain – backpacking should be fun and you should build in easy days and time off to enjoy it.

above: Cycling is a great way of exploring the countryside once you have set up camp and you have the advantage of height so can often spot animals and birds that you might miss if on foot. Hatfield Forest in Essex has over 1,000 acres of ancient woodland and many examples of ancient trees.

Unless you are super-fit, your planning should include getting in better shape. Start by going on long walks and finish up by carrying a backpack full of the stuff that you are going to take.

You also need to plan in order to make a list of what to take. You don't have the luxury of throwing everything into the back of a car; what you need for your trip has to be carried on your back every step of the way. Weight matters so don't plan on taking stuff you don't need and choose what you do take wisely. If you are away for a week you can get by on half a tube of toothpaste, not a full one. This may sound like nit-picking but the more weight you carry, the more tired you will get. The more weight you save, the less you'll have to carry and the more you will enjoy the trip. However, it is always a good idea to bring a couple of days' extra medication with you, in case your return home is delayed, for whatever reason.

Mobile phones can help you keep in contact in most parts of the country but there are still areas where signals are poor or non-existent and bad weather conditions can impact connectivity as well. That is why – if you go out walking alone – you should always leave your itinerary with a friend or family member detailing where you are going, the route you are taking and when you expect to return. It's also a good reason to know how to read a map and use a compass (see pages 70–71) – you can't always rely on the GPS device on your mobile phone!

left: Even with GPS on many phones, it is still essential to know how to read a map and use a compass if you are going to spend a lot of time in remote areas, where you may not have coverage.

WHERE TO GO

The choice of where to go is yours and there is no shortage of choice, whether it is close to the coast, inland lakes, the hills or the open countryside. Do you want sea, sand and sun, to go hiking every day or explore new places? If you like being part of a crowd you can head for a campsite near the beach, which is likely to be busier throughout the summer. If you want some peace and quiet there are still thousands of places tucked away in the heart of the countryside.

What sort of facilities are you looking for? Do you want a campsite that offers evening entertainment or is close to lots of other facilities such as pubs and cafes? Do you want big or small – lots of other campers or just a few? How fussy are you about toilet and shower facilities? Thanks to the internet, you can check out most campsites and their facilities and read reviews from other campers before making any decision.

Britain has so much to offer and you really are spoiled for choice. The following is a very brief look at some of the options available to you.

below: If you have a campervan you can go where you please, especially if the weather turns bad. This classic VW campervan is parked on the cliffs above Kynance Cove in Cornwall.

North West

In the north of England there are magnificent coastlines, the Lake District, historic castles, quaint towns and lots and lots of outdoor opportunities. To the south you have two of the most vibrant cities in the country, namely Liverpool and Manchester, the world's first industrial city. Further south still is the Roman town of Chester, certainly one of the most beautiful cities in Britain with its 13th-century shopping-galleried walkways called the Rows. They get their name because in medieval times each walkway was the domain of a particular

below: The east shore of Derwentwater in summer, looking south to Castle Crag and the 'Jaws of Borrowdale' in the Lake District.

trade – Shoemaker's Row, Ironmonger's Row and so on.

Few places can match the beauty of the Lake District, which has inspired countless artists and poets. The Lake District is England's largest national park covering 885 square miles (2,292km²), with more than a quarter of the land owned by the National Trust, much of which was gifted to it by children's author and farmer Beatrix Potter. Visit the lakeside towns of Ambleside, Bowness, Keswick and Windermere. Enjoy long walks around the lakes or a more leisurely boat trip across them.

Carlisle, just south of the Scottish border, used to be the northern headquarters of the Roman army and the castle was built by William the Conqueror after he seized the town from the Scots. Along the coast are picturesque villages such as Heysham, just south of Morecombe with great views over Morecombe Bay, the largest estuary in the UK. If you want popular beaches head for Blackpool with its attractions and entertainment, and if you are looking for somewhere more secluded, there are tiny coves all along the coast.

above: A 1930s guide book covering the Windermere area of the Lake District at a time when walking and rambling in the countryside were very popular.

next page: These walkers are heading uphill and away from Wastwater, Cumbria. The National Trust campsite at Wasdale Head is just visible to the right-hand side.

North East

The rugged landscapes and coastline of the North East were fought over for centuries by the warring English and Scots. This was the northern frontier of the Roman Empire and one of the power houses of the Industrial Revolution. There are castles and the ruins of fortified buildings on top of many hills, many of them protecting the three major waterways of the rivers Tyne, Wear and Tees. Newcastle is often described as the most vibrant city in Europe – for good reason – although there are many other historic towns to visit such as Alnwick, Bamburgh, Berwick-upon-Tweed, Chester-le-Street and the cathedral city of Durham. When you come across the Bowes Museum at Barnard Castle you could be forgiven for thinking you were in France. The museum is housed in a magnificent French-style chateau.

Berwick is the most northerly town in England with a wonderful castle and famous spired town hall. To the north you can explore parts of the 73½-mile

above: Hadrian's Wall at Hotbank Cragg, Northumberland, is one of the most spectacular sights in the north east of England.

(117km) long, up to 6m (20ft) high Hadrian's Wall built to keep the Scots – or Caledonian Picts – out. The Holy Island of Lindisfarne can be seen off the coast. The first Anglo-Saxon monastery was built by St Aidan in 635AD. Jarrow, in South Tyneside, also dates back to Anglo-Saxon times although it is more famous as a seat of great learning in the 7th and 8th centuries and as the home of the Venerable Bede.

The region is also popular with walkers although it is not unusual to be on a trail for several hours and not see anyone else. You can enjoy upland walking in the Northumberland National Park and the North Pennines Area of Outstanding Natural Beauty.

Midlands

This region is packed with history and architectural jewels from the college towers of Oxford to magnificent Blenheim Palace at Woodstock and quaint Stratford-upon-Avon, birthplace of William Shakespeare. There are the big cities of Birmingham and Coventry offering shopping, historic buildings and entertainment, and the large

above: The 15th-century Courtyard range of Baddesley Clinton. The Courtyard garden was created in 1889 by Edward Heneage Dering with yew topiary and bedding.

town of Warwick – with one of the finest castles in Europe. In the countryside there are beautiful landscaped parks and formal gardens, follies and moated manor houses, such as the 15th-century Baddesley Clinton. Even the names of the villages have a romantic and historic ring to them. Of course, there are also delightful village pubs where you can stop for an excellent lunch or supper before heading back your campsite.

Further north, the Ironbridge Gorge Museums are a World Heritage Site. Then there is the Black Country with its Industrial Revolution heritage and modern attractions such as Alton Towers.

For backpackers there is the Heart of England Way, a 100-mile (161km) long-distance walk that links the Cannock Chase Area of Outstanding Natural Beauty in the north and the Cotswolds in the south. It starts at Milford close to Shugborough Hall and ends at Bourton-on-the-Water. Like most long-distance walks in mainland Britain, it connects with several others including the Beacon Way, Staffordshire Way, Cotswold Way and the Thames Path. There are many campsites along the route.

right: Camping in the countryside allows you to get out and really explore, enjoying stunning landscapes along the way – such as this view across the Brockhampton Estate in Herefordshire.

East of England

This region is most famous for the Norfolk Broads and its fabulous beaches, especially along the north Norfolk coast. On any summer's day there may be more caravans parked in campsites along this stretch of coastline than anywhere else in the country. This is also one of the best wildlife-watching areas in the UK with world-class birding at Minsmere and Orford Ness on the Suffolk coast and migration watching off Blakeney Point.

To the west of East Anglia is the university city of Cambridge with its ancient colleges and wide open spaces – it is one of the few cities that has cattle grazing just a short distance from the bustling market square. Cambridge is one of those cities where you can spend days exploring on foot, either around the colleges or walking along the banks of the river Cam. Other historical places include the cathedral cities of Ely and St Albans, which dates back to pre-Roman times, and Colchester, the oldest recorded town in England.

above: A cigarette card showing a poster by RT Roussel, depicting the pier entrance at 1920s Southend-on-Sea.

The Norfolk Broads, long thought to be a natural feature, are now known to have been created by the Romans digging peat for fuel. This digging continued until the Middle Ages when sea levels rose and the peat pits flooded, creating the shallow lakes or 'brads' that we know today. The swallowtail butterfly (right) is found in the Broads but nowhere else in the UK. The area is also an important habitat for many birds such as the bittern, marsh harrier and bearded tit.

above: The swallowtail butterfly is one of the rare wildlife sights you can see in the east of England.

Southend-on-Sea on the Thames Estuary is a popular resort with seafront arcades and sandy beaches. Further north is the Sunshine Coast, including Great Yarmouth and Lowestoft. Rural and coastal trails offer pleasant walking. The Suffolk Coast and Heaths Path is just one of many worth exploring.

below: A Konik pony at one of the few surviving fenland habitats at Wicken Fen, Cambridgeshire.

South West

The South West is the largest region of England yet has the smallest population. Major cities include Bristol, Plymouth and Exeter, which all prospered as ports. Exeter was also the most south-westerly city in England fortified by the Romans. The region has two National Parks – Dartmoor and Exmoor – and four World Heritage Sites – Cornwall and West Devon Mining Landscape (with its many old mining sites and monuments), Jurassic Coast, Bath and Stonehenge close to the eastern edge of the region. The Jurassic Coast covers 95 miles (153km) of Dorset and East Devon coastline with fossil-bearing rocks up to 185 million years old. The historic Roman city of Bath is on the northern edge of the region and the Cotswolds, with its rolling hills and picturesque, thatched villages, is a designated Area of Outstanding Natural Beauty.

It is a region steeped in history and mythology. The area around Avebury village in Wiltshire is home to some of the most prehistoric monuments in the world, the most famous of which is Avebury Stone Circle. Stonehenge dates back to 2,500BC and much of the north of the area includes Wessex, which was thought to be the home of the legendary King Arthur.

above: As in this 1910 poster, we have a whole world to explore – but why travel overseas when there is so much to see and do at home?

above: There are thousands of miles of wonderful coastal walks around Britain and each one changes with the season, offering different colours, lighting and vegetation – more than enough reason to go back time and time again.

The South West is probably best known, however, for the beautiful tucked-away fishing villages in Cornwall and Devon and the vast areas of open upland and walks that command spectacular views. Because of its scenic beauty much of the coastline is protected from development.

There are tourist areas such as Torquay, Paignton and Weston-super-Mare, but it is the quiet, rural hamlets of thatched cottages and the small fishing villages of stone houses that appeal to most visitors. You can see many of these coastal villages by walking the stunning 630 miles (1,013km) of the South West Coast Path, which runs from Minehead in Somerset all the way round Devon and Cornwall to Poole in Dorset.

South East

The South East stretches from South Berkshire and Buckinghamshire south to the English Channel and then east until you hit the sea again. There are major holiday resorts at Brighton, Eastbourne, Hastings and Worthing. Southampton and Portsmouth are centuries-old naval bases. Portsmouth is home to the world's oldest dry dock still in use and also Lord Nelson's flagship HMS Victory – now a museum and one of the most interesting attractions in the area.

There are the historic towns of Arundel, Chichester, Winchester and Canterbury, and the Isle of Wight, which, because you have to get there by ferry, is almost like going abroad for your holiday. There are several scenic areas such as the New Forest and the North Downs and castles galore with Bodiam Castle in Sussex probably being the most spectacular. Dover Castle sits high above the Channel port on the famous white cliffs and there are spectacular walks along the cliffs. Dover is the end of the North Downs Way National Trail, which runs

below: There are few sights as spectacular as waking early to watch the sun rise or, as shown below, watching a stunning summer sunset from Devil's Dyke in the South Downs of West Sussex.

for 153 miles (245km) from Farnham in Surrey. Other long-distance walks include the 100 mile (161km) South Downs National Trail and the 184 mile (294km) Thames Path – which takes you through the heart of London.

Along the Sussex coast and more so along the Kent coast there are many smaller seaside resorts with camping grounds. Inland there are hundreds of farms growing fruit and vegetables – well worth a detour to go and pick your own.

Scotland

Scotland has it all – beautiful scenery, ancient cities, magnificent wildlife, fabulous food – and even palm trees! It is a near-perfect place for the outdoors enthusiast with walking, climbing, beach combing and a host of other activities. From the rugged splendour of the Orkney, Shetland and Outer Hebrides islands to the history-drenched Scottish borders there is something for everyone.

above: Red deer is among the spectacular wildlife that can be spotted in Scotland.

Edinburgh is a magical place to visit not just because of the castle and its imposing location but because of its history and culture. You can stroll around the ramparts or wander through narrow medieval lanes, enjoy great food, lively clubs and a wealth of cultural events and international festivals. On the west coast is Glasgow with its museums and galleries and incredible architecture. You can also enjoy great food, shopping and a vibrant night life.

Head for the famous Lochs and explore the Highlands or enjoy the seaside at Ayr, which is warmed by the Gulf Stream – which is the reason you can really see palm trees in many towns and villages along the west coast. There are spectacular castles – like Stirling and Glamis – national and wildlife parks, beaches and quant seaside villages. Scotland is also the home of golf and, in addition to the famous course at St. Andrews, there are scores of golf courses, most of which are open to the public.

right: The World Heritage Site, Giant's Causeway in County Antrim, is one of the many must-see sights if you are camping in Northern Ireland.

Northern Ireland

Northern Ireland boasts magnificent scenery, castles, monasteries and historic monuments, beaches, lively cities and a warm welcome that is hard to beat. Belfast is a city that has been transformed over the last few decades and is now a mecca for culture as well as its energetic night life. The walled city of Londonderry can trace its history back thousands of years and has some wonderful buildings showcasing Georgian, Victorian and Edwardian architecture. It also offers great shopping.

Visit Carrickfergus and Enniskillen for their magnificent castles although there are many more to see as well such as Greencastle, Jordan's and Dunluce, which hangs precariously over the clifftop.

There are wonderful natural attractions to explore like the Giant's Causeway in County Antrim – a World Heritage Site – or the Marble Arch Caves in County Fermanagh. Northern Ireland has many large loughs and most are surrounded by historic sites. They also offer great fishing.

Northern Ireland is also a great place for exploring on foot. While the 625 mile (1,000km) Ulster Way is probably too long for most people, there are hundreds of miles of trails through forests, over hills and along the coast. The Mourne Mountain, partly owned by the National Trust, offers wonderful walking during the day but can be an eerie place as night falls, when the mist swirls through the valleys and the fairies come out to play.

Wales

Did you know that there are more than 600 castles in Wales, 750 miles (1,200km) of coastline, three National Parks and five Areas of Outstanding Natural Beauty? Wales is a wonderful area to visit because although it is part of Britain it is very different from its neighbours both in culture and language. North Wales is a walking and camping paradise. Snowdon, at 3,560ft (1,085m), is the highest point in England and Wales – there are six different routes to the top – and is surrounded by magnificent countryside, much of which is owned and cared for by the National Trust. If you don't want to walk to the top, take Britain's only rack-and-pinion railway to the summit. The island of Anglesey has spectacular sea cliffs and secluded beaches and the village with the longest place name in Europe (Llanfairpwllgwyngyllgogerychwyrndrobwllllantysiliogogogoch, which means: St Mary's Church in a hollow of white hazel near the swirling whirlpool of the church of St Tysilio with a red cave). The 12th-century Caernarfon Castle is one of the finest in the principality.

Mid Wales offers beautiful scenery, old farmhouses and wide open spaces. Elan Valley has four huge reservoirs and dams built 100 years ago. At Llanwrtyd Wells you can see some of the most unusual events anywhere – like the Real Ale Wobble and Ramble and the World Bog Snorkelling Championships. Hay-on-Wye, close to the English border, is the book capital of the world. For walkers there is the Brecon Beacons National Park.

The West Coast – Ceredigion – is a place for exploring rocky smugglers' coves and secluded, award-winning beaches. Sit on the edge of the breakwater at New Quay and watch the dolphins and seals. The Georgian town of Aberaeron is famous for its

right: North Wales is perfect for camping with wonderful scenic walks to suit all abilities. In the distance you can see the Watkin Path, one of the six main routes to the summit of Snowdon.

above: Among the pleasures of camping near the coast are the fabulous beaches waiting to be discovered, such as this beach at Whitford Burrows, Gower Peninsula..

local lobster and its honey ice-cream. The National Library of Wales, Aberystwyth, houses many of the nation's greatest literary treasures. Nearby Devil's Bridge is in the foothills of the Pumlumon mountain range.

Southern Wales is the most populated part of Wales but still offers a wealth of historic, cultural and outdoor activities. It is also home to Cardiff, the capital city. Visit the relatively new city of Newport with its strong cultural atmosphere and then on east to the Wye Valley with its many castles, ancient abbeys and fortress towns. Walk the Glamorgan Heritage Coast or explore the many former coal mining valleys that now showcase their rich past at places like the Rhonnda Heritage Park and Big Pit National Coal Museum at the Blaenavon World Heritage Site.

South-west Wales stretches from Swansea and the Gower Peninsula, Britain's first Area of Outstanding Beauty, to the Pembrokeshire Coast National Park with many miles of walking and delightful little towns like Tenby and St Davids. There are hundreds of destinations for a camping holiday by the beach or in the heart of the countryside. Visit Swansea, Wales's second city and the nearby Victorian port of Mumbles. There are castles, such as the imposing Carreg Cennen and Llansteffan, and botanic gardens, including the National Botanic Gardens of Wales, which opened in 2000.

HOW TO GET THERE

If you are setting out for a family camping holiday it makes sense to load your vehicle up with everything you need. Pack the vehicle the night before and try to leave as early as possible to avoid the worst of the traffic. If your destination is only three or four hours away, you could break your journey for a picnic or to go on a walk so that you don't arrive at the campsite too early and have to wait for your site to be ready.

Before heading out, check for travel warnings and weather forecasts. Get a map and make sure you know where you are going. If you are going to be on the road for a couple of days travelling to your campsite but don't want to camp on the way, it is worth having accommodation booked in advance.

TRAVEL GAMES

* Each member of the family can pick a different colour of car and the winner is the first to see ten vehicles of that colour.
* Someone says a word out loud and then everyone else has to come up with a word that rhymes with it. After the first round the next person then comes up with a word and you keep going round until someone gets stumped.
* Memory games are always fun. First select a topic – fruit, for instance. Then the first person says the name of a fruit, the second person has to repeat that fruit and name another and you continue until someone is unable to repeat the complete list. Then select another topic. This is also a great way of memorising useful facts. You could choose rivers of Britain, capitals of the world, kings and queens of England and so on.
* Allocate points for different farm animals spotted. If someone sees a cow, sheep or a pig they get one point for each animal. If the animal is in a herd or a flock they get up to a maximum of ten points. If they see a horse, however, they have to delete two points. So if there are five horses in a field they have to delete ten points. The winner can be either the first one to reach a certain score or the one who has the highest score after a set time limit – perhaps 20 minutes.

above: Illustration by W. Heath Robinson on the front cover of *The Humorist*, May 1939. The Whitsuntide Bank Holiday was one of the few opportunities for people to get out and about in the countryside.

For backpacking trips consider taking the train or bus to get you as close as possible to your destination. There's not much point in taking a car if you are going to park it and then spend the next few days walking away from it. Many trails, even the long-distance ones, can get very busy at weekends and during the summer so if you want some solitude, plan midweek trips if you can, or go in the spring or early autumn.

If you are going on a cycle camping holiday, public transport is also a good way to get you to your destination if it is a long way away – otherwise all you have to do is start pedalling.

above: You may not come across many people as you walk along some of the more remote paths but you will see plenty of wildlife, like this wild mountain goat at Hafod Y Llan farm, Snowdonia.

TRAIL TIPS

* When walking in the countryside stay on the path – ideally the middle of the path. If you walk on the edge or stray off the path, you will cause damage to vegetation and add to erosion. If you are in a group, walk in single file unless the path is very wide.
* If walking in the hills, don't be tempted to take short cuts. If the path zigzags up the hill stay on the path. It might be tempting to cut out a corner and save a few steps but by leaving the path you will damage the environment. The National Trust spends millions every year repairing footpaths in the Lake and Peak Districts.
* Keep noise to a minimum. Noise disturbs the peace and quiet of the countryside for others. In addition, if you make too much noise, you will frighten any wildlife away and see nothing.
* Respect any wildlife that you do see. Observe silently from a distance.
* Keep dogs on a lead and under control at all times.

SETTING UP CAMP

The ideal campsite is grassy, flat, well drained and sheltered. Even if you have been designated your camping spot when you arrive at the campsite, you should always check out the area before erecting your tent. Make sure there are no sharp stones or broken glass that could tear the tent and no large rocks that might dig into you as you sleep. Make sure there is no discarded food around, which might attract animals and insects. Which way do the prevailing winds blow? You don't want them buffeting the tent all night. Pitching near a hedge provides shelter. If you are camping in a wooded area, are there any branches hanging over your tent? Apart from pine trees that can drip sap, you could have problems with birds roosting and leaving deposits on your tent and around the campsite. If there are storms, water will continue to drip on to your tent from overhanging branches long after the rain has stopped.

Do you want to camp close to the amenity block? It may be convenient for night-time visits but if you are too close you will get a lot of foot traffic close by.

right: Choosing the right campsite is important not just to be safe but to enjoy the best panoramic views possible. Every time you come out of the tent there should be a 'wow' as you take in all the beauty around you. Wasdale Head in the Lake District is one of the most scenic campsites in the UK.

HOW TO PITCH A TENT

Pitching a tent is always easier when there are two people and it is much more straightforward if you have put it up before. Earlier I mentioned that you should always practise putting up your tent in your back garden after buying it – not only see how to do it but also to check that you are not missing any vital parts.

When arriving at a campsite erecting the tent should be the first task – and ideally while it is still light so that you can check the ground first for sharp objects and so that you can see what you are doing. Clear the ground of anything that might damage the tent or dig into you while you sleep. Make sure you are not in a hollow because if it does rain heavily you could finish up with quite a lot of water in your tent. It is also best to pitch the tent on grass or other natural ground cover rather than bare earth because, if it does rain, the area will not get too muddy.

Check to see if the land slopes – even slightly. If the ground is flat that is fine but if there is a slope you will probably want to pitch the tent so that you sleep with your feet pointing down the slope.

It is best to lay the tent out on the ground and push the tent pegs in first before inserting the poles. Make sure the tent is stretched out to its full extent in all directions – this will ensure maximum space inside. Not all tents need pegs but even if you are using a freestanding tent, it is still a good idea to use pegs for added security.

Most poles are made of aluminium, galvanised steel, fibreglass or carbon fibre. A few are still made of wood but other materials are

right: When you get to a campsite, pitching the tent should be the first thing on your agenda. Once it is up you can get the kettle on and make a nice hot drink.

above: Guy ropes and pegs, like these used at Brownsea Island in Dorset, are important for tent stability but make sure they are not a hazard to you or people passing by.

lighter, stronger and more durable. Aluminium poles tend to be used on larger tents because they provide more rigidity – although they can bend in very strong winds. Fibreglass poles tend to be sectionalised and connected together by shock-cords, so that they almost spring together during assembly.

Be careful when inserting poles through sleeves in dome tents and similar. It is easy to tear the material if you try to force the poles through. Also, don't bend the poles excessively as they can snap. Attach the flysheet if it comes separately and, finally, peg out any guy lines, making sure they are taut.

GUY LINE TIPS

Check all guy lines regularly to ensure they stay taut and, if bad weather is expected, add extra guy lines or use rope to secure the tent to a tree, fence or your vehicle. Make sure everyone in your party is aware of where the guy ropes are – you don't want people tripping over them and hurting themselves and maybe damaging your tent.

SAFE CAMPFIRES

First, are campfires allowed at the campsite? If they are, that is great because there is nothing like sitting round a campfire swapping stories at the end of the day. Also, food cooked on a campfire tastes so much better.

Before building or lighting any fire, however, some basic safety precautions have to be taken. If it is windy, what is the danger of stray sparks igniting a wildfire? What is the surrounding area like – is there a lot of tinder-dry undergrowth that could catch alight? Are there branches overhead that could catch alight if the fire flares up?

Some campsites have fire rings or fire pits – designated areas where fires can safely be lit. You may be able to build a ring of rocks to contain the fire but always use non-porous stones that will not shatter if they get hot.

If you light a campfire don't store extra wood too close and don't build the bonfire into a blazing inferno, which could quickly get out of control. Campfires

below: Sitting round a campfire – like this one at Highertown Farm in Lansallos, Cornwall – swapping stories under the stars, is one of the great pleasures of camping and creates memories that last a lifetime.

should be small and contained so that they are easy to control. It is also a lot easier to sit round a small fire and enjoy each other's company without sparks flying everywhere or smoke getting in your eyes. Even though the bonfire may not be large, always have water nearby to douse flames.

Building a campfire is a skill and one that all campers should learn. Campfires should only be built when there is a supply of available dry, dead wood. Do not pull branches down or strip bark off trees. Some campsites sell bundles of firewood for this purpose. If you are near the beach you can gather driftwood that has washed up and then dried above the high-water line.

A campfire consists of three elements – tinder, kindling and fuel. Tinder can be dry leaves or grass, small dead twigs or balls of cotton wool (always good to keep some in a plastic bag for emergencies). If you expect wet weather and still need to light a fire, you can soak the cotton-wool balls in lighter fuel and store them in a waterproof container so they stay dry and do not contaminate other items.

Kindling consists of slightly larger twigs, strips of paper twisted together and anything else that will burn. Tinder is used to get the fire started and kindling builds up the heat until the flames are ready to tackle the larger pieces of wood, which is to be the fuel.

Fuel wood should never be thicker than your arm otherwise it will be difficult to break and take too long to burn, as the fire should only be alight for the time you need it. Don't leave a fire unattended.

If it is windy you can protect the fire by using a sleeping mat or flysheet as a windbreak. This will prevent the fire flaring up or burning too quickly.

Before going to bed make sure the campfire is completely out. Kicking earth over the embers cannot be guaranteed to put them out. If necessary, pour water over any smoking embers to extinguish them.

right: Marshmallows toasted on the end of a twig over a roaring campfire are truly yummy and provide a great dessert.

STAYING SAFE

Nobody wants to have an accident but they do happen and often at the most inconvenient times and in the most inaccessible places. However, good planning and basic common sense can prevent most mishaps.

Wearing sensible footwear prevents slips, the most common type of walking accident, resulting in sprained ankles and worse. Grass is slippery after rain or heavy dew and wet rocks and muddy paths can be a hazard. Never walk too close to the edge of a cliff – you can't be sure how stable the ground is. Never cross a flooded river or stream until you know how deep it is. If you have children, explain to them why it is not safe to run around the campsite as they might trip over tent pegs or, worse, fall into the fire.

No matter how comfortable your trainers or boots are while walking it is a good idea to stop every two hours or so to take them off and shake them out. The smallest piece of dirt can rub your foot until you get a blister.

Even though you are camping, you should always practise good hygiene. Wash your hands frequently and use hand sanitiser sprays.

Use insect repellant to prevent bug bites and sun screen so that you don't burn. Keep tents closed to stop insects getting in and don't use a torch when entering or leaving as this will act as a beacon and attract them.

Bugs and animals are also attracted by food, so don't leave things out and always clean up any spills. If you have left-over food pack it in plastic containers that will trap any odours. If you want a fry up for breakfast, pour the fat into your fire pit and burn it when you light your campfire. Discard any cans or food packaging materials into receptacles provided by the campsite.

Always have a well-stocked first-aid kit with you (more on this on pages 72–73) and, more importantly, know how to use it. It's a great idea to sign up for a first-aid course before you go camping – the knowledge you gain will be invaluable and could help save lives.

BASIC SURVIVAL

Through no fault of their own people can find themselves in survival situations – being caught in a fierce snowstorm, being trapped by flood water or taking a bone-breaking tumble while walking in the hills. That is why everybody who goes into the countryside should have several basic survival skills because one or more could, in an emergency, save your life.

Of all survival skills, basic first aid is probably the most important. Would you know what to do if someone was bitten by an adder (don't panic but consult a doctor) or stung by a jellyfish (rinse; remove remaining tentacles)? If you are miles from anywhere and one of your group breaks an ankle, could you cope?

Survival skills include first aid, map reading, use of a compass, building a basic shelter, lighting a fire, foraging for food, finding drinking water and knowing how to conserve heat and energy. Not only are these skills important to learn, they will also come in useful time and time again, and considerably enhance your enjoyment of the countryside. It is a satisfying feeling to know that you can probably cope with most things that could happen to you or your family.

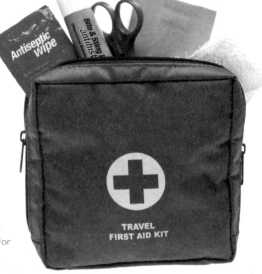

right: Whether you are backpacking or family camping, a first aid kit is essential. For backpacking you just need the essentials but if you are family camping, pack for all eventualities – see pages 72–73 for what to pack.

Map reading and orienteering

Map reading is not practised as much as it used to be because of the availability of GPS devices, either stand-alone or built into mobile phones, but it is still an important skill to possess. Always make sure you have the most up-to-date version of any map.

You can get so much information from looking at a map apart from just knowing where you are. If one of your party is injured, a map will show you where the nearest habitation is and how best to get there. The shortest route may not always be the best one if it involves hiking down the side of one hill and up another when one of your party has sprained an ankle, and you can find that out by consulting the map. If you are out on an exposed hill and storm clouds are

right: All backpackers should carry a map and a compass – and know how to use them.

below: One of the pleasures of backpacking is being able to get away from it all – and that often means navigating areas not visited before – that's when a map and compass are essential.

gathering, you can study the contour lines on the map to find a spot that will provide you with the most shelter from the elements.

You should be able to orientate the map using landmarks to determine in which direction you are heading. It is always best to pick three or four landmarks to be certain. The map's legend will help you identify features you may not be sure about.

Orienteering comes into its own when you are travelling through woods or don't have great visibility. You should be able to read the map to see where trails bend or fork because that helps locate your position.

Using a compass

The advantage of a compass is that it is quick, accurate and can be used under all weather conditions and in any terrain.

A compass can greatly assist both map reading and orienteering – provided you know how to use it. If you are following your route on the map and see a prominent landmark ahead that is in your line of travel you can take a compass bearing on that object. If you then descend into trees and can no longer see the landmark you can still follow the compass bearing to lead you to it. If you are in a group walking through trees you can still stay on course using the compass, provided you know the bearing to follow. One person holds the compass to determine the right course and another person sets out in that direction until he or she is almost out of sight. The group then walks to that point and you repeat the process. It is slow but steady and a lot better than getting lost in the woods. The same method can be used to navigate at night.

What should a basic first-aid kit contain?

If you are camping as a family and working from a base you should have one comprehensive first-aid kit that you can keep in your vehicle close to the campsite as well as a smaller basic kit that you carry in your day pack when you go on outings and walks. Remember also to pack all prescription medicines that you and family members need. If you are backpacking, every member of the group should have their own first-aid kit in case you get separated.

The most common minor accidents are cuts and scrapes but if you have a campfire or are cooking there is always the danger of burns.

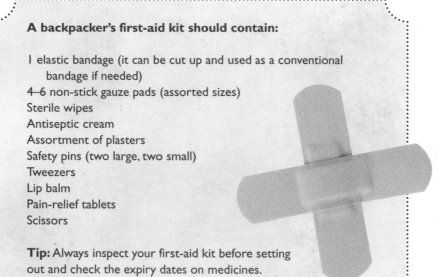

A backpacker's first-aid kit should contain:

1 elastic bandage (it can be cut up and used as a conventional
   bandage if needed)
4–6 non-stick gauze pads (assorted sizes)
Sterile wipes
Antiseptic cream
Assortment of plasters
Safety pins (two large, two small)
Tweezers
Lip balm
Pain-relief tablets
Scissors

Tip: Always inspect your first-aid kit before setting out and check the expiry dates on medicines.

Many campers carry a knife so scissors may not be necessary. All of these items can be packed in a small, clear, waterproof plastic bag, which enables you to see and then extract what you need quickly.

The family first aid kit should contain:

Assortment of plasters
2 x 5cm (¾ x 2in) and 2 x 10cm (¾ x 4in) bandages
Assortment of butterfly closures – for closing small
    wounds and lacerations
Elasticated bandage for sprains
Roll of medical tape
Assortment of non-stick gauze dressings
Moleskin and liquid skin – for blisters
Antiseptic cream
Antiseptic cleansing wipes
Sterile wipes
Disposable gloves
Cotton-tipped swabs
Safety pins
Scissors
Tweezers
Thermometer
Eyewash cup

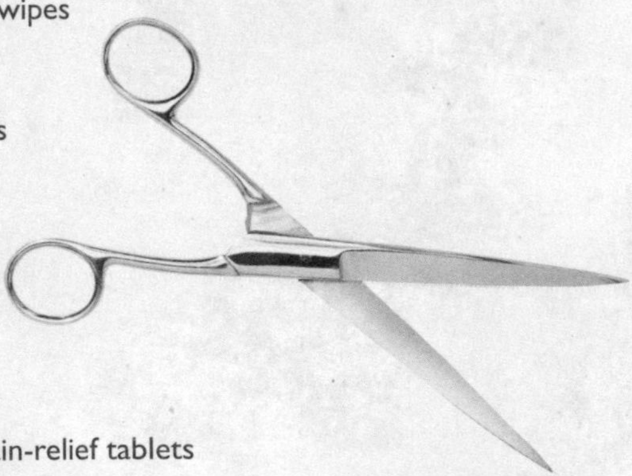

Plus:
Aspirins or other pain-relief tablets
Sunburn-relief gel
Insect-bite relief gel, spray or wipes
Anti-diarrhoea tablets
Lip balm
First-aid booklet

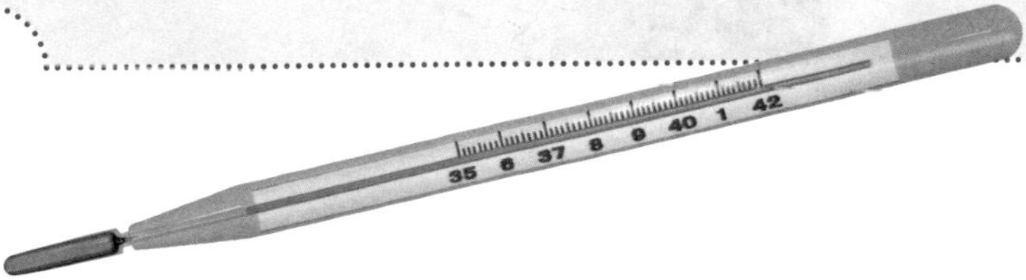

BASIC FIRST AID

Cuts, scrapes and bruises

There are several types of cuts including incisions, lacerations, punctures and abrasions. Incisions are caused by sharp objects such as broken glass or a knife and the skin on either side of the cut can usually be pulled together. Lacerations are jagged cuts, such as when you trip and fall on to a sharp rock. Abrasions (scrapes) are usually superficial wounds only affecting the top layers of skin. It often looks bad – and hurts – but it is not serious.

In all cases, clean the area with a sterile wipe, apply antiseptic cream and, where possible, try to keep the skin intact and close the cut as much as possible. Cover with a plaster or bandage. For bigger cuts and open wounds use both a wet and dry gauze pad. The wet gauze pad goes on the wound so that when it is removed it will not stick. The dry gauze pad goes on top of the wet pad and both are held in place with a bandage. Always apply the pads directly on to the wound – don't slide it on to the wound and make sure the pad completely covers the wound on all sides. Clean open wounds at least twice a day.

Puncture wounds are caused by being pierced with a long thorn or similar object. Clean

above: Always carry a first aid kit because even a small scratch or cut can become infected if not treated properly – and that could spell disaster.

the puncture mark and cover with a plaster but inspect regularly because these wounds can get infected if bacteria is lodged below the skin.

Bruises will usually heal on their own but if they are the result of a sprained ankle, arnica cream, ice packs and leg elevation will help reduce the swelling.

Sprained ankle

Remember RICE for Rest, Ice, Compression and Elevation. Don't try to remove footwear because this allows the ankle to swell rapidly. Make sure the injured person stays off their feet and rests the ankle. If you have access to ice on a campsite apply it and then use an elastic bandage to apply compression – not too tight – to keep the swelling down. Elevate the foot.

Insect bites and stings

Some people are acutely allergic to insect bites and stings and can go into anaphylactic shock, which requires immediate medical attention. Even if you are not allergic, multiple stings or bites can still be extremely painful. Clean the affected area carefully and gently with soap and water – bees leave their sting embedded in the skin, which may cause further contamination – and apply some antiseptic ointment.

If you have multiple, very itchy insect bites, wet the area and then gently rub an aspirin tablet over the bites. Aspirins contain an anti-inflammatory agent that will reduce the itching. Calamine lotion and baking soda are both effective in reducing swelling and itchiness from bites.

For bee stings remove the stinger immediately. Scrape your fingernail along the skin to get between it and the stinger and then flick it out – never try to squeeze it out. All the time the stinger stays in it will pump more toxin into you.

If you are stung by a jellyfish, vinegar will help neutralise the sting.

Stinging nettles can give you a very itchy rash but a cold compress or a rub with a dock leaf brings quick relief.

Snake bite

Adders love dry, open heathland and moors, and like to bask in the sun – usually on a footpath – but if it is very hot they like to stay cool in damper areas. Adder bites are not common and they will only strike if they feel threatened. The chances of being bitten by a snake are extremely slim but if you are concerned, especially if you have children, you can buy a snake-bite kit. It is large suction cup that fits over the bite and literally sucks the venom out. In any event, you should seek medical attention as quickly as possible after a snake bite.

Burns and sunburn

Minor burns can be treated with anti-bacterial ointment and covered. For more serious burns you should seek medical attention.

When sunbathing, of course the best thing to do is not to get burned in the first place. Use suntan cream or lotion and make sure the children are protected – especially on those areas that are not usually exposed to the sun.

If you are sunburned, calamine lotion and aloe vera can both soothe and cool. Milk can also be used – soak a cloth in milk and lay it across the affected area or dab milk-soaked cotton balls on the burns. The tannin in cold tea may also reduce the inflammation – dab the area with tea bags.

For serious sunburn with bad blistering it is worth consulting a doctor as anti-inflammatory medications might be needed. If you are staying on a big campsite the first-aid office can tell you what needs to be done.

Water safety

Everybody loves the water when the weather turns warm and a little thought about water safety can ensure everyone has fun – and stays safe at the same time. If you have very young children, keep an eye on them at all time. If you go into the water it is always a good idea to go with someone else. That way you can help each other if necessary.

Another important lesson is to know your limits. If you are not a good swimmer don't go into water that is too deep or too rough. Always be able to keep your feet on the bottom. Only swim in safe areas and if a lifeguard is on duty swim where he or she can see you. The best safety tip of all, however, is to learn to swim. Teach children how to swim as early as possible.

St John Ambulance offers a free pocket-sized guide that gives essential first-aid advice. It covers five common conditions for which straightforward first aid could be the difference between a life lost and a life saved. You can order your copy at their website: www.sja.org.uk.

above: Beaches are fun places but care is still needed, especially if you have young children. Too much sun can ruin a holiday and everyone should know basic water safety.

SECTION TWO:

CAMPFIRE COOKING

COOKING AROUND THE CAMPFIRE

B ritain's diversity of beautiful scenery is only equalled by its enormous variety of regional cuisines – almost certainly more than any other country of comparable size. From Dundee cake and Scottish salmon to Cornish pasties and Devon cream teas, there is an enormous choice of mouth-watering foods to choose from.

There is no doubt that British food has been much maligned by people from other nations for many years, yet this reputation could not be further from the truth. We have the freshest of produce and an enormous choice of quality meat, fish, fruit and vegetables.

One of the great pleasures of camping in different parts of the country is that you get the opportunity to sample the very best of locally grown produce. You can do a big shop in the nearest town but it is so much better to support

the local growers close to where you are camping. Farmers' markets and farm shops offer fresh produce, which can be used to prepare quick, nutritious, healthy and very tasty meals. Even better, go out and pick your own fruit and vegetables wherever possible. It's not only a great way to spend an hour or two – picking and sampling – but you get the freshest of produce at below farm-gate prices.

Many of the recipes in this section can be made from produce bought at farm shops or pick-your-own farms and will give you a taste of the best of British!

left: The old kitchen kettle can boil water over a campfire but there are lots of new cookers that will do the job quicker and use less fuel.

above: Nothing beats a fried bacon and egg breakfast when camping and even the coffee seems to taste better out of doors.

Just to give you an idea of what is in store – literally – here is a rapid dash around the country:

Scotland has lots to offer from fresh trawler-landed deep-sea fish to salmon and trout straight from the loch or fish farm. There are hearty breakfasts and thick nourishing stews made from local oats and barley – all great for providing the energy needed for long walks in the hills. While on the hills you will probably spot game – deer, pheasant, partridge and grouse – all of which can be bought locally in season. Scottish cheeses are excellent, such as the traditional Caboc, and there are many newer home-produced cheeses that you are unlikely to find in the shops outside the region. Some of the best berries can be found in Scotland, especially raspberries and tayberries.

above: Foraging for fungi, like this child at Attingham Park in Shropshire, is a great way to learn more about nature – and by selecting the right mushrooms, to add some local flavour to your meals.

The North East produces some of the country's finest sausages – great for campfire meals. There are also wonderful cheeses such as Wensleydale and Chevington; speciality breads such as stottie cake and ginger parkin. Yorkshire lays claim to some of the best fish and chips in Britain and for those who like their fish a little stronger, there are smoked Craster kippers from Northumberland, which are said to be a favourite of the Queen.

The North West gives us Lancashire Hot Pot and wonderful shrimps and other shellfish, farmhouse cheeses – especially Cheshire (reputed to be England's oldest cheese) and Lancashire – and delicious fruits and vegetables. For quick snacks and decadent desserts there are all sorts of buns and pastries specific to the area such as Chorley, Eccles and Simnel cakes and gingerbreads from the Lake District.

above: Scotland is rightly famous for its game birds – from partridge and grouse to the spectacular pheasant – all of which can be bought and enjoyed in season.

Wales offers a fine range of speciality cow and goats' milk cheeses from Caerphilly to Llanboidy. There are locally grown fruits and vegetables and, for the more adventurous, there is laver bread, made with edible seaweed, which is an excellent breakfast accompaniment to Welsh farm-cured bacon. The long coastline and rivers also provide plenty of fish, especially trout, and the salt marsh lamb is delicious. Welsh cawl is a traditional stew made of lamb, leeks, potatoes and carrots although ingredients can vary from region to region. It is the ideal one-pot meal as it was traditionally cooked in a large cauldron over an open fire. It was served as two courses – the first being the broth from the pot and the second the meat and vegetables.

The Midlands are often called England's bread basket because it provides so much of the country's food. It is famous for its fruit and vegetables and a wide

range of dairy products from cheeses to yoghurts and speciality farm-made chocolates. There are also excellent meats – lamb, beef and pork – and, of course, pork pies. Local bacon is perfect for a hearty camping breakfast while cakes such as Staffordshire fruit cake, Banbury cakes or Shrewsbury biscuits are a delicious way to finish a meal.

The East of England extends from the borders of the Heart of England east to the North Sea, taking in the East Midlands and East Anglia and a huge variety of regional and local food specialities. There are lots of local cheeses to try – red Leicester, sage Derby and of course Stilton, the king of cheeses. This fertile area produces vegetables, fruit and berries, and the coastline provides a variety of shellfish, including the delicious Cromer crab.

above: Blackberries, whether growing wild or gathered on a pick-your-own farm, make fabulous desserts.

The South East includes Kent the 'Garden of England' and other vast areas of rich, fertile farmland, which produce an abundance of vegetables, fruit and dairy products. There are many pick-your-own farms where you can gather apples, cherries, pears and plums and a wide array of berries. You may be lucky and find a wild hazelnut or cobnut tree. The extensive coastline provides fish and shellfish – from the famed Dover sole to jellied eels.

The South West is probably best known for its cream teas and abundance of seafood. Dairy farms produce wonderful cheeses – such as Cornish Yarg and mature Cheddar – and clotted cream. The surrounding seas provide a rich harvest of fish and shellfish. Cornish pasties are a great trail snack, as are apples, which can be eaten raw, cooked or drunk with your dinner after they have been made into the local cider!

Of course, Britain is also famous for its puddings – Spotted Dick for instance. Bread-and-butter pudding, treacle tart, plum pudding and many more both fill you up and pack in the calories needed for energetic days in the countryside.

above: With the exception of France, Britain has probably more cheeses than any other nation, and camping around the country allows you to sample the many wonderful regional specialities.

DID YOU KNOW?

There are scores of different types of English sausage, and bangers and mash remains a favourite meal for many people. Sausages became known as bangers during the First World War. Because meat was scarce butchers added more water to the mix, which turned to steam during cooking, causing the sausages to burst open with a loud bang.

Cornish pasties have been made for almost 300 years and were originally baked for the tin miners who worked deep underground in filthy conditions. The pastry was wrapped around beef, sliced potato, swede and onion, and was so thick that it stayed warm for several hours. By lunchtime, however, the pasty was pretty dirty so the miners ate the contents and threw the pastry away. Thankfully, today you can eat it all.

Pork pies also have a long and colourful history and can lay claim to being one of the oldest known 'packaged' foods. The origins of the pork pie date back to medieval times and they were said to have been taken by the knights going to the Crusades. As with the Cornish pasty, the pork-pie pastry was mostly used to protect the meat contents and was often uneaten.

NUTRITION TIPS

Food provides the energy needed for the body to function. Even if a healthy adult male spent all day in bed, he would still need around 1,000 calories a day to keep his body functioning without losing weight. And the more you do, the more you can eat.

Normally about two-thirds of calories are used to maintain body temperature and keep the heart, muscles and other organs functioning properly; the rest are used for working or exercising.

If we eat more than the body needs, the surplus is converted to fat. This goes back to prehistoric times when our early ancestors gorged whenever there was plentiful food, in order to build up reserves to survive during times of shortage. Today, we do not need to gorge but many of us still do, which is why getting out and exercising, especially walking in the countryside, is such a good idea.

The harder a person works or exercises, the greater the number the calories that are needed. A coal miner used to need up to 5,000 calories a day; a modern office worker needs about 2,000; and a mountaineer up to 8,000 calories. If you are planning on a 20-mile (32km) day hike with a 13.5kg (30lb) pack over reasonably difficult terrain, you probably need to pack in 5,000 calories or more.

Understanding basic nutrition helps you plan your meals so that you – and your family – get the right balance of protein, carbohydrate, vitamins and so on, so that your body can function efficiently and you stay healthy.

The body consists of about 70 per cent water, 15 per cent fat, 12 per cent protein and a few other bits and bobs! Muscles are composed almost entirely of water and **protein**, which is why it is important to eat protein every day to allow the body to repair and rebuild new tissue. Adult meat eaters need about 85g (3oz) of protein and vegetarians about 140g (5oz) a day from other sources. Because children are still growing, their protein requirement for body building is much higher, at two to three times the adult intake.

Despite their bad rap, the right **fats** are important because they provide essential fat-soluble vitamins. However, fat can only be metabolised if the body has carbohydrates to start the conversion process. Fats also make us feel full, which signals the brain to stop eating.

Carbohydrates (carbs) are the real energy providers. Starches and sugars are broken down and stored mainly in the liver and muscle as glycogen. When the body needs energy, the glycogen is converted back to glucose, the 'fuel' needed to drive and heat muscles. The advantage of carbs as an energy giver is that they can be reconstituted without the need for significant oxygen so if you are on a long hike with plentiful glycogen you should be fine. It takes about 10 per cent more oxygen to release energy from fat, which means there is less oxygen available to pump through muscles and you tire quicker and will get cramps. When you run out of accessible fuel, this is known as 'hitting the wall' and it takes enormous willpower to continue. The best solution is to consume complex carbohydrates, found in less processed foods, which take longer to break down and give a more controlled blood sugar release.

The amount of **vitamins** we need to take in depends on the level of activity being pursued. For very physical activities it is a good idea to increase your intake of the B vitamins as these are needed to convert carbs into usable sugars. They also help build stamina. Vitamin C is necessary because the body can neither produce it nor store it – so eat lots of fresh fruit and vegetables. Lack of vitamin A leaves you vulnerable to infections and vitamin K helps with blood clotting.

Minerals, even in tiny quantities, are essential and lack of them can cause many medical problems. Calcium is needed for healthy bones and teeth and iron for the synthesis of haemoglobin, which pushes oxygen around the body. Other essential minerals are sodium, potassium, magnesium, phosphorus, chloride and iodine. A special group of minerals, the '**electrolytes**' are lost through sweating. If too many electrolytes are lost while exercising, the first signs are usually muscle cramps and then severe muscle contractions.

Fibre or 'roughage' comes mostly from vegetables and is necessary for bowel regularity – important if camping. Perhaps that is why baked beans have always been so popular as a campfire dish. Fibre also makes you feel full.

Liquids are hugely important. Physical exertions over a day's hard hill walking can cause you to lose several pounds in weight and valuable minerals and electrolytes – these must be replaced as soon as possible. Dehydration in hot weather can sometimes lead to heatstroke.

All of the above elements have an important role to play as part of a balanced diet, which is why it is important to plan your meals carefully, whether going away for a family weekend or heading off into the hills to walk from John O'Groats to Land's End.

The more we understand about what we should eat and how much of it, the healthier and fitter we will become and, therefore, the more enjoyment we will get when we visit the countryside.

PLANNING AND PACKING FOR THE CAMPING KITCHEN

If you are hiking, everything that goes into your pack should be used while you are away. If you don't need it, why carry it? However, if you are getting ready to go on a family camping trip and everything is going to be loaded into the car or trailer – not on your back – you have a lot more freedom when you are choosing what to take.

Planning for the camping kitchen involves two stages – what you are going to eat and what you will need to take to prepare it.

I mentioned earlier the importance of working out a meal plan for your trip. This should include breakfast, lunch and dinner for each day as well as snacks, drinks and treats. You don't necessarily have to stick rigidly to this plan – you can have Tuesday's dinner on Friday night if that is what you fancy. Or you might see something while you are away in a farm shop or local store that looks so good you buy it for that night's meal.

The advantage of writing out a menu is that you can make a list of all the other ingredients you will need for each meal and get them pre-packed. Remember your favourite herbs and spices, sauces and all the other things that you will use in creating your chosen dishes.

right: The farm shop at Chirk Castle in Wrexham is signposted in both Welsh and English. An increasing number of National Trust properties are opening shops selling a wide array of fresh, local produce.

far right: Farm shops allow you to be truly creative when it comes to cooking. Rather than shop with a recipe in mind, see what is on offer and then create a menu around it.

EQUIPMENT, STORAGE AND COOKING METHODS

Apart from your camping stove, you will need pans, lids, a kettle and a frying pan. If you are planning on cooking over a campfire as well, you will need a grill to sit your pans on – you could bring the grill from your barbecue at home.

Plastic plates, bowls, mugs and glasses are safer as they don't shatter and are sturdier than glass. You can get some very elegant plastic wine glasses for those dinners under the stars. If you are bringing a camping table to eat at, why not bring along a tablecloth as well and have your meals in style?

A small folding table – such as a card table – provides a firm base for preparing meals and can be stowed away when not needed. You will also need a cutting board and sharp knife for food preparation.

Other utensils include large wooden spoons for cooking and serving (they don't get hot), a non-stick spatula, measuring cups, colander, tin opener and that all-important corkscrew.

Two of the most useful items to have are aluminium foil and ziplock plastic bags. The foil can be used in campfire cooking, for keeping cooked food warm and for wrapping up leftovers and lunches. Strong, ziplock bags can be used to store ingredients and leftovers. You can also use them to marinate steaks or to toss chicken breasts in flour.

Basic items are flour, cooking oil, tea, salt and pepper, coffee, hot-chocolate powder, sauces and

left: Making a brew is the easiest and often the most enjoyable cooking chore of the day. Nothing beats a warm cuppa first thing in the morning.

above: Use large wooden spoons for cooking and serving, like this wooden ladle, which do not get too hot to handle while cooking and are easy to dry in the sun.

other condiments, stock cubes, sugar or sweeteners, rice, spaghetti – and whatever else you and your family use on a regular basis.

You will also need a bowl for washing up, soap or washing-up liquid (preferably biodegradable), a scouring pad, dish cloths, paper towels (for napkins and mopping up spills, which you can then burn in a campfire) and rubbish bags. Don't forget to bring matches to light your fire or stove.

A cool box is a great idea if the weather is hot and you are able to buy ice. The cooler can protect your most perishable foods although if it is very hot you should plan on using perishable foods as quickly as possible.

You will also need something to collect and store water. Collapsible buckets are great for backpackers but on a large campsite where the water taps may be some way away, a large plastic container that can be wheeled is best.

A battery-operated camping lantern is useful if you want to prepare after-dark snacks. Remember, however, that if you use the lantern in the dark you might quickly be surrounded by moths and other nocturnal insects.

BUILDING A CAMPFIRE

Cooking over a campfire is fun and certainly enhances the taste of the food and the camping experience. There is a difference, however, between a campfire for sitting around and telling stories and a campfire for cooking.

The secret of a good campfire for cooking is to get all the wood turning to hot embers at about the same time. This prevents flare-ups, which can be dangerous, and the embers will provide you with a constant heat while you cook. First find two large pieces of wood or stones and place them on either side of where you plan to light your fire. Use tinder and kindling to get the fire started and then fuel it with pieces of wood about the same size. Distribute the wood evenly over the fire. Once the wood has burned to white embers you can divide them into two piles – one thicker than the other. The thicker pile will provide more heat and can be used for cooking, while the smaller pile can be used to keep food warm. Once you have separated the embers, put a grill over the fire so that it rests on the logs or stones on either side. You place your pans on the grill and move them around to get the desired heat – hot or warm. You are now ready to start cooking. To stop the supporting logs from burning, douse them with water every now and then.

Don't try and make a tripod of sticks over a blazing fire and suspend your cooking pan from it. Flare-ups from the fire will make it impossible to get an even temperature and the bottom and sides of the pan will be so blackened it

left: Toasting marshmallows is great fun for all the family – a forked stick works equally well if you don't have a toasting fork to hand!

above: An early 20th-century design from an Ogdens cigarette card showing two Boy Scouts in camp cooking an evening meal over the campfire.

above: The embers of the campfire make a great oven – and a great way of baking foil-wrapped potatoes. Other vegetables, meats and fish can be cooked in the same way.

will take forever to clean it. Above all, this sort of construction is very unstable and just the act of stirring the saucepan's contents – trying to avoid the flames – could cause everything to collapse into the fire.

After you have finished cooking, you can add more wood to the fire and build it up into a regular campfire to sit around.

This type of cooking campfire also gives you enormous versatility. You can wrap potatoes and other root vegetables in foil and bake them in the embers of the fire. You can wrap thick slices of meat in cabbage leaves and roast them in the hot embers. The cabbage leaves do not burn and the meat stays wonderfully moist. There are all sorts of other exciting ways to experiment with campfire cooking. You can even bake chocolate cake in camp – using an orange. You hollow out an orange; half-fill the inside with chocolate-cake mix, wrap everything in foil and cook on the fire for about ten minutes. The result is delicious helpings of chocolate cake.

You can use a Dutch oven (a very heavy cast-iron casserole with three legs) on or in an open fire. It can be used as a griddle – turn the lid over for frying eggs and bacon – and as an oven, frying pan or roasting dish. It can even be used to bake fresh bread every morning! Embed the oven in the hot embers and pile more on top of the lid to create the right temperature for baking. Always use an oven with short legs that can straddle the embers – the utensil should never be in direct contact with them. When buying a Dutch oven, choose one that has handles on both the base and lid, and make sure the lid has a raised edge so that embers will stay on top and not slide off. You can get lighter aluminium Dutch ovens but it is more difficult to regulate the heat and, besides, if you are transporting the Dutch oven in the car the extra weight is less of a problem. Needless to say, if the Dutch oven has been standing in the fire it is going to get very hot. Take great care when removing the lid or the pan and use thick oven mitts. If the Dutch oven is full of food it will be very heavy so it is best to slide a thick stick through the base handle so that two people can lift it off the fire.

above: Large pots and pans are great for family camping, especially when cooking over an open fire. A grill is a great accessory as it provides a stable base for your pots.

NATURE'S FREE LARDER

You get so much more out of a camping trip if you are able to identify the flora and fauna around you. After rain, it is fun looking at tracks that have been made by various animals and birds and trying to identify them. If you don't know what made a particular track, draw a picture of it or make a plaster cast (for details of how to do this, see page 163) and try to identify it later from reference books. Making plaster casts is an easy and fun activity for all the family.

Later in the book (see pages 150–153) you will see how you can predict the weather by observing animals, birds and plants. You can also supplement your camp kitchen with a host of goodies if you know the right things to pick from nature's abundant free larder.

I am not advocating the wholesale destruction of everything edible in the countryside but with a little thought and a little more knowledge there is no reason why campers should not only know more about nature but also let it work for them. Leaves, berries, nuts and fruits can be picked, but plants should never be uprooted or destroyed in the process or stripped bare.

There are scores of shrubs and plants that can be harvested and enjoyed. Many are also highly nutritious. Young tender nettle leaves can be cooked and eaten like spinach (but take care when picking them). Chickweed, with its small yellow-green leaves, is rich in iron and can be eaten raw, added to salads or cooked. Yarrow, one of the most common of all wild flowers, can also be cooked in water and eaten as a green vegetable. In olden days, couples getting married carried a bunch of yarrow because it was supposed to ensure lasting happiness. Shepherd's purse, ground elder and lungwort also make excellent green vegetable stand-ins.

left: Gathering fungi is fun but always rely on an expert to tell you what is edible and what is not!

Herbs that add garlic flavours, such as Jack-by-the-hedge, or more subtle flavours such as balm and rosemary are all found in the wild.

Everyone knows the dangers of eating poisonous toadstools and mushrooms, but there are many varieties of edible fungi to add to the cooking pan and some that can turn a meal into a feast. Consult a field guide for more details on which mushrooms are edible and which are not (see Further Reading, page 204). The rule is, of course, don't pick anything unless you are absolutely sure of what it is. If in doubt, leave it out.

Edible seaweeds make delicious vegetable accompaniments and wild herbs can spice up a campfire meal. Seaweeds are at their best when picked during the summer months and, of course, there are shellfish and fish that are good to eat.

Shellfish can be eaten all year round although it is best to avoid them during very hot weather – those months without an 'r'. Only gather living specimens, wash well and cook quickly. You can tell if a specimen is alive by trying to open

below: Humans have been picking blackberries for thousands of years – and over that time I am sure the pickers have always eaten as many berries as they have collected.

the shell – if it is alive, it will quickly shut itself again. If the shell is open or does not close, leave well alone.

There are usually no restrictions on gathering seaweed or shellfish from the sea but you should check local bylaws and always check to see if a license – either freshwater or saltwater – is needed to catch fish. You will need a rod license and then may need a separate license or landowner's permission. Local fishing-tackle shops are the best place to inquire.

Clams can be dug out of the sand near the low-water mark. Mussels are best gathered as far into the sea as possible and should be boiled for at least 20 minutes, long after the shells have opened. Always remember when gathering shellfish to keep an eye on the sea – don't get trapped by a fast-incoming high tide and make sure that mussels are harvested away from any water pollution.

Late summer and autumn provide rich pickings with nuts, berries and other fruit. There are hazelnuts for snacking and sweet chestnuts to roast in the campfire. Wild strawberries while small are delicious, as are wild plums and blackberries. Other fruits such as crab apples may not be as sweet but they are still nutritious – and free.

Nature's larder truly is abundant and the more trees and plants that you are able to recognise, the more pleasure you will get from your trips into the countryside, especially if you return to the same areas frequently. You may be out camping in the spring and recognise a walnut tree or spot a dense thicket of brambles. Make a note, because when you come back in the autumn there will be nuts and berries for the picking.

MEDICINAL PLANTS

For centuries, wild plants and herbs have been used to treat ailments in the countryside and some of these remedies can still be very useful today. The leaves of blackberries for instance can be used to cure diarrhoea, dandelion leaves are a natural diuretic and plantain leaves – chewed to soften them up – can be rubbed on insect bites to relieve the swelling and pain.

above: Picking blackcurrants in the Kitchen Garden at Knightshayes Court in Devon. Blackcurrants are not only delicious they are good for you – rich in vitamin C and said to be effective in preventing colds, soothing sore throats and relieving the symptoms of arthritis.

RECIPES

TRAIL SNACKS

Energy bars make great snacks any time, but especially after a few hours' walking when you need a little boost. Some of these bars can be made at home while others can be made at the campsite. If wrapped in foil they should last for up to two weeks – although there will rarely be any left for that long!

Mixing the ingredients for energy bars can be messy but is still best done with your hands.

Granola nut bar

Preparation and cooking time: 10 minutes

Ingredients:
750g (1lb 10oz) peanut butter (smooth or crunchy)
680g (1½lb) honey
250g (9oz) porridge oats (uncooked)
285g (10oz) protein powder
90g (3oz) raisins
30g (1oz) wheat bran

Combine the peanut butter and honey in a saucepan and warm over a medium heat – stir often – until blended and smooth. Put porridge oats, protein powder, raisins and wheat bran in a large bowl and mix together, then add the peanut butter and honey mixture, and stir until everything is completely blended.

Spread the mixture out on a sheet of greaseproof paper and greased baking tray, and allow to cool. Cut into slices. You should be able to get at least 16 average-sized bars. Wrap them individually and store in the fridge until needed.

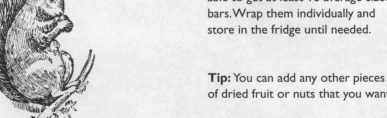

Tip: You can add any other pieces of dried fruit or nuts that you want.

Bouncy bars

Preparation and cooking time: 30 minutes

Ingredients:
2 eggs
170g (6oz) brown sugar
2 teaspoons vanilla extract
285g (10oz) granola
115g (4oz) chopped mixed nuts
170g (6oz) raisins or mixed dried fruit
170g (6oz) chocolate chips

Combine the eggs, sugar and vanilla extract in a bowl and blend thoroughly. Mix in all the remaining ingredients.

Spread out evenly on a well-greased baking tray and bake in a preheated oven at 180°C/350°F/Gas 4 for 20–25 minutes.

Remove from the oven and allow to cool. Cut into required bar sizes.

Tip: One of the fastest ways of producing a delicious energy food that all the family will enjoy is to remove the core of a ripe apple and fill the hole with a mixture of peanut butter, mixed nuts and raisins. If you want to take this snack on the trail just wrap it in foil until you are ready to eat it.

right: Lightweight pots cook food faster so you use less fuel and they are a lot easier to carry.

Crispy oatmeal cookies

These cookies are thin and crispy rather than chunky and chewy. Thinner is healthier, and less likely to get messy if your cookies get warm on the trail.

Preparation and cooking time: 20 minutes

Ingredients:
170g (6oz) brown sugar
100g (3½oz) granulated sugar
230g (8oz) butter
2 large eggs
1 teaspoon vanilla essence
200g (7oz) plain flour
1 teaspoon baking powder
Salt (optional)
250g (9oz) porridge oats

Beat the sugars and butter together until creamy. Mix in the eggs and vanilla and then slowly beat in the flour and baking powder (and salt if preferred). Add the oats and blend in thoroughly.

Use a rounded tablespoon full of mixture as your cookie measure and place on a baking tray. Bake in a preheated oven at 180°C/350°F/Gas 4 for 12–15 minutes. Check the last few minutes of baking to make sure the cookies don't burn but the longer you cook them the crisper they will be.

You can add all sorts of extras to the mixture if you wish – raisins, chocolate chips, dried fruit and so on. A teaspoon of cinnamon added with the flour also imparts a distinctive flavour.

Chocolate balls

Preparation and cooking time: 20 minutes

Ingredients:
50g (1¾oz) butter, softened
250g (9oz) crunchy peanut butter
50g (1¾oz) Rice Krispies
170g (6oz) dark chocolate chips
115g (4oz) icing sugar

At the campsite:
In a large bowl, combine the softened butter and peanut butter, then add the Rice Krispies, chocolate chips and sugar and mix thoroughly. Use a spoon to scoop out the mixture, roll into balls and pack separately.

At home:
As above, but do not add the chocolate chips. Instead, melt the chocolate chips and butter in a pan then dip the balls making sure they are completely covered in the melted chocolate. Place on a baking tray and cool in the fridge.

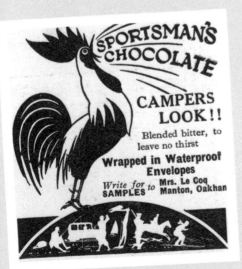

left: A 1930s advertisement for Sportsman's Chocolate from *The Hiker and Camper* magazine.

BREAKFASTS

Eggs 'n' coffee

This is a very practical – and fun – way to start the day. By making your eggs and coffee at the same time you can save fuel as well.

Preparation and cooking time: 10 minutes

Ingredients (serves 2):
4 eggs
2 tablespoons water
Salt and pepper to taste

You need a strong plastic bag that can withstand boiling. Crack the eggs into the bag and add salt and pepper and water. Seal the bag and shake to combine the ingredients. Fill a pan with water for your coffee (or tea) and as it comes to a boil drop in the plastic bag. After 2 or 3 minutes, take the bag out to see if the eggs are cooked. There shouldn't be any liquid in the bag. If necessary, give the bag another shake and return to the water for another minute or so. The scrambled eggs will be super light and fluffy.

Lord Montagu of Beaulieu told me many years ago that the secret of great scrambled eggs was to add water not milk – try it and see for yourself.

left: Campfire coffee always seems to taste so much better than when you drink it at home – another of the many pleasures of camping.

Yummy pancakes

There are many variations of this recipe — add bananas for healthy, fruity pancakes or sauté up some onions and green peppers for a savoury Tex-Mex breakfast.

Preparation and cooking time: 10–15 minutes

Ingredients (for 12 pancakes):
285g (10oz) flour
2 tablespoons sugar
1 teaspoon salt
1 teaspoon baking powder
2 eggs
480ml (16fl oz) milk
60g (2oz) butter
1 tablespoon oil

Filling:
1 chopped banana
or 1 onion, finely chopped and
1 green pepper, finely chopped

Mix together the flour, sugar, salt and baking powder. In a separate bowl combine the eggs, milk and butter and then blend in the flour mix to make your batter. Finally, add the sliced bananas (or onion and pepper) to the batter.

Heat a frying pan over a medium heat, coat the bottom with a little oil and pour in about 2 tablespoons of batter; cook, turning the pancake carefully when the bottom is golden brown.

Serve with a dollop of farm-made strawberry jam if you are having the banana pancakes.

left: Take the opportunity to buy fresh local produce whenever you can. It will probably taste better and be cheaper than the produce you buy back home.

Bannocks

Bannock is a flatbread that has been made in Scotland and Ireland for many centuries. It was said to be a favourite of Queen Victoria. The surprise is that you can make bannock in less than 20 minutes while camping so there is no excuse not to have fresh bread. The original bannock was unleavened bread but by adding baking powder it becomes much lighter and you can add whatever other ingredients you like into the mix. Raisins, berries or currants transform it from bread to cake.

Preparation and cooking time: 20 minutes

Ingredients:
500g (1lb 2oz) flour (or potato flour)
2½ tablespoons baking powder
1 teaspoon sugar
½ teaspoon salt
1 tablespoon butter
Water, as needed

Mix all the dry ingredients and stir together. Add half the butter and slowly add water while stirring until you have a firm dough. Melt the remaining butter in a large frying pan (just enough to stop the dough sticking) and then add the dough, pressing it into a round shape. Depending on the thickness of the dough cook for 6–8 minutes until the bottom is golden brown. Flip it and continue to cook for another 6–8 minutes on the other side.

Allow to cool a little and serve while still warm. The best way to eat bannock is to tear it apart into chunks, which are great for mopping up juices or gravy on your plate. Bannock is also delicious spread with butter and jam or honey.

QUICK AND NUTRITIOUS LUNCHES

Summer soup

This is another recipe that allows you to go and pick the freshest of vegetables from the local shop.

Preparation and cooking time: 15 minutes

Ingredients:
4 vegetable or chicken stock cubes, made up to 2 pints (40fl oz)
Potatoes, carrots, tomatoes, onions, celery, mushrooms and anything else you want to add
1 sprig of parsley
Salt and pepper to taste
Crusty bread, to serve

Fill a large pan with the vegetable (or chicken) stock and add the chopped vegetables and parsley. Bring to the boil for about two minutes and then simmer for a further 8–10 minutes, stirring occasionally. By sipping a spoonful every now and then you can also season to adjust the taste. The vegetables should be *al dente*, not mushy. Serve with fresh crusty bread, to mop up the last drops.

If you have other leftovers – meat, rice or pasta – you can throw them all in for a more hearty meal.

below: Farm shops and local markets offer a wide range of fresh produce which you can incorporate into your camping recipes.

Sizzling stir-fry

*The beauty of stir-fry is that you can add whatever you like so it makes
a great meal towards the end of your camping trip when you want to use
up a lot of leftover ingredients.*

Preparation and cooking time: 10–15 minutes

Ingredients:
This meal can be made with
ingredients from local farm shops –
onions, tomatoes, mushrooms, carrots,
peas in their pods, peppers, broccoli
florets and whatever else is available.
Meat lovers can cut rashers of bacon
into strips or use thin strips of
chicken breast. If the chicken strips are
thin enough the meat will be cooked
thoroughly as long as you keep turning
it during cooking. For a little
crunchiness you can add some
unsalted roasted peanuts.

Stir-fry sauce:
2 tablespoons soy sauce
(the low salt variety is best)
1 tablespoon Worcestershire sauce
1 tablespoon cornflour
1 tablespoon brown sugar
120ml (4fl oz) red wine or
cider vinegar
120ml (4fl oz) water
2 large garlic cloves, crushed
Ground black pepper to taste

Combine all the ingredients in a large, sealable plastic bag. If you want a little
more zest you can add ½ teaspoon of cayenne pepper and 1 teaspoon of
ground ginger. This produces a thick soy sauce packed with flavour. If you prefer
a runnier sauce, add 240ml (8fl oz) of chicken stock. If you are having stir-fry for
lunch, mix all your ingredients after breakfast and let them marinate and mature
for a few hours.

Preheat the pan for about a minute before adding the oil – just enough to
cover the sides and the base with a thin film and no more (don't preheat if using
a non-stick pan).

Chop or slice all the vegetables (and meat) into bite-size pieces – it is best
to shred the carrots – and add to the pan. Add a little water if necessary
(although there should be enough from the vegetables), and stir-fry for 3–4
minutes. Remember that onions take longer to cook than most vegetables so
keep these in the centre of the pan so they get the most heat initially.

Push the vegetables to the sides and add the stir-fry sauce to the centre of the pan so that it can thicken a little before mixing it with the other ingredients. Then simmer (covered if possible) for another 3–4 minutes.

Serve with fresh crusty bread if this is for lunch. If you want to have this for dinner, serve with quick-boil rice or noodles.

If you want to add thin strips of beef, cook these first and then remove to cook your vegetables. When you add the sauce, you can put the beef back to heat through again. By cooking the meat separately you will not overcook it, and both the meat and the vegetables should retain their own flavours.

Tip: It's better to stir-fry in a wok because the sloping sides don't get as hot as the base. This means that you can move vegetables to the side once they have been sautéed and continue cooking other ingredients in the centre of the wok.

right: Buying from farm shops not only guarantees the freshest of fresh, you can often find special breeds of poultry and local varieties of fruit.

Camping pizza

These camping pizzas are made with flour tortillas, which make for a delicious crust that almost melts in the mouth. Lots of people like their pizza 'loaded' with as many toppings as possible but the secret of a good pizza is to keep the ingredients to a minimum – tomato sauce, mozzarella and then two ingredients that really go well together. This way each ingredient can be tasted and each taste blends harmoniously with the others. My favourite combinations are blue cheese and sliced pears, lean bacon and pineapple and chicken and BBQ sauce.

Preparation and cooking time: 10–15 minutes

Ingredients:
Tomato or pizza sauce
1 large tortilla per person
Toppings of choice – mushrooms, onions, peppers, sliced courgette, salami, pepperoni and so on
Mozzarella cheese
Vegetable or olive oil
Parmesan cheese (optional), for sprinkling on after cooking

Spread a thin layer of pizza sauce on the tortilla, arrange your toppings and cover with a thin layer of mozzarella cheese.

Use enough oil on the bottom of a frying pan to prevent the pizza from sticking. Heat the pan until it is very hot and then add the pizza with its toppings. Heat until the cheese is nicely melted.

You can also use pitta bread in the same way although the cooking time will be a little longer.

Tip: If you are cooking by campfire, you can spray a large sheet of foil with oil – it must overlap the tortilla by at least 10cm (4in) all round. Prepare the tortilla as above and place in the centre of the foil. Use a second tortilla to cover the first. Then place a second piece of foil over this and seal using the overlap. The pizza in its foil is then cooked over the flames using the grill. It takes 10–15 minutes to cook the pizza this way so you can all share a slice while the next one is cooking.

Farm-fresh salad

Salads are quick, easy and healthy and they don't have to be boring! You can try all sorts of grated fruit and vegetables in addition to lettuce, cucumber, radish, tomatoes and spring onions. If broccoli and cauliflower is in season you can use florets of those to add to your mix.

Preparation time: 10 minutes

Ingredients (serves four):

2 large cooked chicken breasts cubed
1 large lettuce (dark-leaved lettuce varieties have more nutrients)
45g (1½oz) fresh spinach leaves
2 large carrots, grated
Tomatoes, cucumber, radishes, celery, spring onions, prepared as usual
60g (2oz) grated Cheddar cheese or blue cheese (according to preference)
60g (2oz) mixed nuts and fruits (berries, raisins and so on)
30g (1oz) black olives (without stones)
Sliced hard boiled eggs (optional)

Dressing:

3 tablespoons olive oil
2 tablespoons balsamic vinegar
½ teaspoon dried oregano
Salt and pepper to taste
If you like garlic you can add it and if you want a little more sweetness, add a pinch of sugar

You may have a favourite family salad dressing but this is an easy one to make and is very tasty. Blend well, pour over the salad and mix in.

PERFECT PICNICS

Pasta salad

If you want this dish for lunch, prepare the pasta and peas after breakfast and allow them to cool down. If the weather is hot, it is best to store the pasta in a cooler or ice box until you are ready to use at lunchtime.

Preparation and cooking time: 20–25 minutes

Ingredients (serves four):
455g (1lb) dried pasta (penne, shells, rigatoni or similar)
140g (5oz) fresh peas
4 medium fresh tomatoes, diced
2 sticks celery, chopped
1 bunch spring onions, finely chopped

Boil a pan of water and add the pasta and peas – an easy way to cook them together. Cook the pasta until it is *al dente* (usually 8–10 minutes). Allow the pasta and peas to cool completely. Add the tomatoes, celery and spring onion to the pasta and toss.

You can serve this pasta as it is or add cubes of cooked chicken breast, prawns or even lobster meat if you can buy them locally.

Farmhouse sandwiches

Freshly baked bread and farm produce make delicious and nourishing sandwiches and you can be as adventurous as you like.

Preparation time: 5–10 minutes

Sandwiches can be open or closed and fillings can be hot or cold. Cold fillings include lettuce, tomatoes, mushrooms, cucumber, onions, cheese, eggs and watercress as well as meats, fish and prawns. Hot fillings can be fried mushrooms, tomatoes, bacon and sliced ham as well as hard-boiled eggs and melted cheese. Sliced smoked salmon open sandwiches with warm scrambled eggs or sliced hard-boiled eggs are delicious.

above: William Heath Robinson's front cover of *The Humorist*, April 1938. Two exhausted cyclists sleep off a picnic lunch, unaware that somebody is riding away on their tandem bicycle.

Stuffed pancakes

Normally pancakes are served hot but this recipe allows them to cool down – which they do very fast outdoors. So as one person makes the batch of pancakes someone else can stuff them – and you can all then sit down and eat together.

Preparation and cooking time: 20 minutes

Ingredients (serves four):
115g (4oz) plain flour
2 eggs
200ml (½ pint) milk
75ml (2½fl oz) water
50g (1¾oz) butter
Fresh lemon wedges

For the fillings:
Your choice of fillings will depend on your personal tastes and what you can get fresh locally.

You can mix fresh fruits such as raspberries and strawberries with clotted cream.

You can have cooked prawns and cream cheese or a mixture of cottage cheese with slices of apple and pears.

Add the flour to a bowl, make a hole in the middle and crack in the eggs. Use a fork to start mixing. Then gradually add the milk and water and keep mixing until the batter is smooth.

Melt the butter in a frying pan, get the pan very hot and add 2 tablespoons of batter. Swirl the batter around the pan so that it is evenly spread and cook for about 25–30 seconds. Use a knife to inspect the underside. If the pancake is golden – as it should be – flip it over and cook for a further 10 seconds or so. Remove and repeat the process until you have enough pancakes.

Stuff the pancakes with your desired mixture, fold over or roll up, sprinkle with lemon juice and serve.

Chicken orchard delight

Preparation time: 15–20 minutes

Ingredients (serves four):
60g (2oz) plain yoghurt (you can use low fat if you wish)
60g (2oz) mayonnaise
1 teaspoon lemon juice
1 teaspoon curry powder
2 large cooked chicken breasts, sliced
2–3 large apples, cored and sliced (we like to keep the skin on)
1 stick of celery, chopped
Fresh crusty bread

In a large bowl, blend the yoghurt, mayonnaise, lemon juice and curry powder. Add the chicken, apple and celery and mix thoroughly.

Spread on fresh bread and eat either as a closed or open sandwich.

right: Apples collected in a swill, or basket, in the garden at Wordsworth House in Cockermouth, Cumbria.

DELICIOUS ONE-POT DINNERS

One-pot dinners allow you to cook several ingredients together, saving fuel (and washing up) but still providing you with a tasty and nutritious meal.

Fast fish stew

Preparation and cooking time: 30–35 minutes

Ingredients (serves four):
About 1.5kg (3lb 5oz) fresh trout or 1kg (2¼lb) trout fillets (or salmon)
900ml (1½ pints) water
4 large potatoes, sliced
1 large onion, sliced
1 stick of celery, diced
1 fish stock cube
Pinch of allspice (optional)
270ml (9fl oz) single cream
2 tablespoons butter
Pinch of dill (optional)
Salt and black pepper, to taste

Prepare the trout (or salmon); make sure all bones are removed and cut into large pieces.

In a large pan add the water, potatoes, onion, celery, crumbled fish stock cube and allspice (if using).

Over a medium heat bring to a simmer, cover and cook for about 15 minutes – until the potatoes are soft. Add the fish and simmer for a further 15 minutes. Do not allow the liquid to boil as the fish will quickly disintegrate into flakes.

When the fish is cooked, remove from heat, mix in the cream, butter, dill (if using) and black pepper and serve with fresh crusty bread. Like many of the recipes in this book, bread is a great accompaniment. There is surely nothing finer than fresh bread and it helps you soak up anything you can't get with your spoon.

Potato curry

Preparation and cooking time: 30 minutes

Ingredients (serves four):
Vegetable oil
4 large potatoes, peeled and diced
150g (5½oz) cauliflower florets
1 large onion, sliced
2 large cloves garlic, crushed
1 tablespoon curry powder
½ tablespoon ground ginger
2 tablespoons malt vinegar
1 tablespoon mango chutney
4 medium tomatoes, chopped
240ml (8fl oz) vegetable stock
Salt and pepper, to taste
Fresh parsley, to garnish

Warm the oil in a large frying pan, then add potatoes, cauliflower, onion and garlic. Cook until the garlic is golden. Add the curry powder, ground ginger, vinegar, chutney and tomatoes and cook for a further 3–4 minutes. Stir in the vegetable stock and season to taste. Cover and simmer for about 20 minutes.

Garnish with some chopped parsley and serve.

below: Good preparation and planning can eliminate many of the tedious cooking chores of old.

Potato, ham and cheese stew

Preparation and cooking time: 20–25 minutes

Ingredients (serves four):
1 tablespoon margarine
1½ teaspoons flour
240ml (8fl oz) milk
Salt and pepper, to taste
230g (½lb) chopped ham
2 large potatoes, peeled and sliced thinly
1 large onion, finely chopped
1 tablespoon breadcrumbs
60g (2oz) Cheddar cheese, grated

In a large pan, melt the margarine and add the flour and mix into a paste. Slowly add the milk, mixing all the time until the sauce thickens. Season with salt and pepper to taste.

Add the ham, potatoes and chopped onions and cook in the sauce for about 15 minutes.

Sprinkle the breadcrumbs and cheese on top and cook for a further 5 minutes until the cheese has melted.

Tip: This is such a quick and tasty dish you can even serve it for breakfast – simply add some fried or scrambled eggs and you'll be all set for the day. If serving for breakfast you can substitute bacon for the ham.

left: Early potatoes grown at Trehill Farm in Pembrokeshire, Wales.

Corned beef hash

This is a hearty meal that you can tailor to your own tastes.

Preparation and cooking time: 20 minutes to boil the potatoes, 10 minutes to cool them and then 25 minutes to make a hash of things!

Ingredients (serves four):
2 large potatoes
2 tablespoons vegetable or olive oil
1 large onion, peeled and sliced
340g (12oz) tin corned beef, cubed
3 tablespoons Branston-type pickle
3 teaspoons Worcestershire sauce
Salt and pepper to taste
Green salad and crusty bread, to serve

Cook the potatoes (we don't peel the potatoes because we think it gives the dish more flavour and texture), allow to cool and then dice.

In the same pan, warm the oil, add the onions and cook for two minutes.

Add the potato and fry for another 5 minutes until the onions are brown and the potatoes crisp.

Add the corned beef, pickle and Worcestershire sauce, season to taste and cook for 10 more minutes. Once everything is bubbling away don't stir so that the underneath can get nice and crisp. Use a knife to turn an edge up to make sure it is not burning.

Turn the hash over and cook for another 5 minutes to allow the underside to get brown and crispy as well.

Serve with a crispy green salad and chunks of fresh bread.

Vegetable supreme

This is another recipe which allows you to improvise as much as you want. The ingredients can vary depending on what is available locally. I like to chop up cauliflower, onion, carrots, celery, tomatoes, runner beans, mushrooms and whatever else is to hand.

Preparation and cooking time: 25–30 minutes

Ingredients (serves four):
Small head cauliflower
1 large onion
2 carrots
2 large sticks celery
4 ripe tomatoes, skin removed
Large handful runner beans
2 large garlic cloves, crushed (optional)
230g (8oz) fresh mushrooms
2 tablespoons vegetable or olive oil
1 litre (1¾ pints) water
230g (8oz) Cheddar cheese, grated
Salt and pepper to taste
230g (8oz) thick cream

Chop all the ingredients into slices or small pieces. Melt the oil in a large pan and sauté the onions until soft. Add the water and remaining vegetables; bring to a simmer and cook for 10 minutes. Stir in the grated cheese until it starts to melt.

Season to taste and serve with a large dollop of cream.

If you want to bulk up the meal add spaghetti. Break the spaghetti in half and, if it is the one-minute cook spaghetti, drop it in the pan just before you add the cheese.

Tip: Instead of using all water you can use 700ml (1¼ pints) water and 115g (4oz) tomato paste, or you could use a large can of cream of mushroom soup to substitute for the mushrooms and cream.

Sausage-with-anything stew

I have been lucky enough to travel all over the world but the one thing that I always miss is a good British sausage. The Americans have their hot dogs and little breakfast sausages, the Germans have their wurst, the Spanish have chorizo, but no one makes a sausage that can compare with the great British banger.

Preparation and cooking time: 30 minutes

Ingredients (serves four):
8 sausages, cut into good-sized pieces
480ml (16fl oz) vegetable stock
4 tomatoes, skinned and chopped
1 large onion, sliced
2 medium potatoes, sliced
140g (5oz) peas
140g (5oz) carrots, sliced
1 teaspoon Worcestershire sauce
1 tablespoon plain flour
8 tablespoons water
Salt and pepper to taste
… and anything else you want to add

In a large pan or frying pan brown the sausages and drain off any excess fat. Add the stock, the tomatoes and all the vegetables and simmer gently for about 15 minutes. Add the Worcestershire sauce and simmer for a further 5 minutes or so until the potatoes are cooked.

While the vegetables are cooking, mix the flour and water into a paste. When the potatoes are cooked, add the flour mix and stir until the stew thickens (you don't have to add the flour mix because the stew will be fine without it but it does thicken the stew up nicely). Season to taste.

Tip: You can also wrap strips of bacon around the sausages.

left: You can cook wonderful, gourmet meals on a camp stove but it is still hard to beat a plate of sizzling British bangers.

Chicken in the pan

Preparation and cooking time: 30 minutes

Ingredients (serves four):
1 tablespoon vegetable or olive oil
4 skinless chicken breasts, each cut in half
240ml (8fl oz) chicken stock
2 large potatoes, diced small
2 large carrots, cut into small strips
Salt and pepper, to taste

Heat the oil in a large pan, add the chicken and brown. Add the chicken stock and vegetables; bring to a simmer and cook for 15–20 minutes. Season to taste.

Tip: Add fresh sweetcorn to gives a whole new dimension to the dish.

above: Buy fresh free range poultry from local farm shops – it has so much more flavour than factory farm raised chickens and turkeys.

NO-POT DINNERS

Tin-foil treats

Preparation and cooking time: 15–20 minutes (times will vary depending on the heat of the embers – if the food is not cooked, wrap it up again and put it back in the fire).

Ingredients (serves 2):
4 carrots
2 small onions
2 small potatoes
1 tablespoon vegetable or olive oil
2 burgers (beef, chicken or turkey)

Cut all the vegetables into small pieces and divide into two equal portions. Take a large square of aluminium foil and in the centre drop 1 teaspoon of oil.

Place a burger on the oil and put the vegetables on top. Take opposite corners of the foil and bring together, repeat with the other corners and twist all 4 ends together to seal the pouch. Drop into the embers of the campfire and cook. Make two.

There are lots of variations of this recipe – all of which involve steaming the ingredients inside the foil. You could use chunks of chicken and pineapple pieces with some strips of green pepper, or pork pieces with slices of apple.

Tip: A useful way to know when the burger is cooked is to wrap the foil in a wet paper towel and then wrap this in a second piece of foil. When the paper is dry the meal is cooked. This way you can inspect the paper to see if it still wet without disturbing the contents in the inner pouch.

Fresh fish 'n' chips

I hate to admit it but the best fish and chips I have ever had was in Canada! I was camping with a Cree Indian called Percy along one of the lakes in the Hunter Narrows of northern Saskatchewan. We had been fishing all morning and he had caught some perch and a trout – I caught nothing. At lunchtime we paddled to the shore, lit a wood fire and Percy chopped the fish into pieces, dropped them in a pan and then sliced potatoes on top of them. The finishing touch was a generous sprinkle from his 'herb' bag, which he kept in a leather pouch on his belt. The lunch was fantastic. I am not sure if the following recipe can beat it but it comes a very close second.

Preparation and cooking time: 25 minutes

Ingredients (serves four):
4 fish fillets
4 large potatoes
4 tablespoons olive oil
Salt and pepper
Fresh parsley, to serve
2 lemons, cut into wedges

Tip: You can substitute prawns or lobster instead of the fish or have all three for a feast.

Make sure the grill is completely clean. This prevents the fish from sticking and from being tainted by anything that was cooked earlier. Make sure the fish is liberally covered with oil – to prevent sticking – and don't be tempted to turn the fish every few seconds. If you do, it will disintegrate long before it is ready to eat. Finally, don't sprinkle salt on the fish before cooking as this will dry it out.

Cut the potato into thick slices (so they will not break up during cooking), coat with oil, sprinkle with pepper and place on the hot grill. Cook for about 15–20 minutes turning every 5 minutes or so until the outsides are crispy and the insides still soft.

Brush the remaining oil over the fish and cook for about 3–4 minutes each side. The cooking time will depend on the thickness of the fish. If necessary, stack the potatoes on a cooler area of the grill while the fish is cooking so that they do not overcook. Season and serve with a little parsley and lemon juice.

right: There is no finer fish to eat than the one you caught yourself but even if you don't catch anything, fishing is a great way to enjoy nature and the countryside.

Fish in foil

This is another quick and easy way to prepare delicious fish on the grill.

Preparation and cooking time: 20 –25 minutes

Ingredients (serves four):
4 boned fillets, such as trout, perch or salmon
2 tablespoons olive oil
2 teaspoons black pepper
2 large cloves garlic, crushed
1 large onion, sliced
4 small potatoes
Dabs of butter
2 lemons, cut into wedges

Brush the fillets with oil and season with pepper and garlic. Place each fillet on to a large square of foil. Cover with onions and fold the edges of the foil up to make a sealed pouch.

Cut each potato into slices without going all the way through. Insert dabs of butter into some of the slits, sprinkle oil over and wrap up the potato. Repeat for the remaining potatoes.

Place all the foil packages on the grill and cook for 10–15 minutes. The great thing about steaming the fish in this way is that you trap in all the flavours, you do not mess the grill up and it is very hard to overcook the fish. Serve garnished with lemon wedges.

Rustic lamb

This is a very quick and tasty way of creating your own sweet-and-sour BBQ dishes. You can use almost any meat instead of lamb – chicken breasts, drumsticks, pork chops or you could even try sweet-and-sour sausages for something really different.

Preparation and cooking time: 10 minutes

Ingredients (serves four):
4 decent-sized lamb chops – more if they are small or you have a big appetite
Salt and pepper
English mustard
White sugar

Trim excess fat off the chops, although leave some as it adds flavour. Sprinkle one side of the chops with a light dusting of salt and pepper. Apply an even layer of mustard and then sprinkle with sugar. Lay sugar-side up on the grill and cook for about 2 minutes, turning only once. Turn the chops over, season, add mustard and sugar to the top and cook until done – about 2 minutes or less depending on the thickness of the chops. It is always best to cook them medium-rare to start with because you can always do one or two a little longer if necessary to suit personal preferences.

Serve with salad and crusty bread or potato or with cold pasta or potato salad.

left: Lambs and sheep in the fields of the Stourhead Estate, Wiltshire.

Super salmon

Salmon is a delicious food and an easy fish to barbecue. If you are cooking for children, make sure you remove any bones before serving. Because salmon has a very delicate flavour it is important that the grill is clean before cooking. This will also prevent the fish from sticking to it.

Preparation and cooking time: 40 minutes

Ingredients (serves four):
2 tablespoons lemon juice
4 tablespoons pineapple or orange juice
4 salmon steaks with the skin on (choose the size according to appetite)
2 tablespoons brown sugar
4 teaspoons chilli powder
2 teaspoons grated lemon rind
½ teaspoon ground cumin
½ teaspoon salt
2 lemons, cut into wedges
Green salad, to serve

Place the lemon and pineapple or orange juice in a large, sealable plastic bag. Add the salmon and shake to coat the fish with the juices. Allow to sit somewhere cool for at least 30 minutes.

In a bowl mix the sugar, chilli powder, lemon rind, cumin and salt; rub half the mixture on one side of the fillets and place on the hot grill. Cook for 3–5 minutes, depending on size (see below). Turn; rub the rest of the mixture on the top of the salmon and cook for a further 3–5 minutes. When cooked the fish should flake easily. Serve with lemon wedges and green salad.

When barbecuing salmon a good rule of thumb is to cook 100g (3½oz) fillet for about 3 minutes on each side, and a 200g (7oz) fillet or steak for about 5 minutes each side.

Tip: If you want to cook your salmon with a barbecue sauce apply it thickly when you put the salmon on the grill. Cook for 3–5 minutes, turn it over, apply more sauce and cook for a further 3–5 minutes. Remove from the heat, allow to cool for a couple of minutes and then remove the skin, which should come off quite easily.

Another tip: A fun way of barbecuing whole cleaned salmon or other fish is to wrap it in newspaper. Scrape the scales off and make sure the innards have been removed. Season the inner cavity with salt and pepper, and give all the outside a good coating of oil.

Open up the newspaper and spread some fresh parsley and basil on it, then place the salmon on top.

Roll the newspaper up tightly and tie off the ends so that the salmon is sealed in. Wet the newspaper thoroughly and then put it on the hot grill. Turn it after about 20–25 minutes and grill for another 20–25 minutes. The newspaper may well start to char but the soaking should prevent it from catching alight.

When cooked, unroll the newspaper and serve. Just like the old days when you had fish and chips out of newspaper!

Hearty grilled chicken

Preparation and cooking time: 45 minutes

Ingredients (serves four):
4 boneless, skinless chicken breasts
4 tablespoons olive oil
2 tablespoons lemon juice
2 tablespoons orange juice
1 tablespoon Worcestershire sauce
30g (1oz) freshly chopped basil
2 cloves garlic, finely chopped
Salt and pepper, to taste

In a bowl mix all the ingredients together, apart from the chicken. Dip the chicken breasts in the mixture so that each is thoroughly coated and then put the breasts in a sealable plastic bag to marinate for about 30 minutes. Marinate for longer if you can keep everything nice and cool, in a cooler box for example.

Fire up the grill and when it is hot, add the chicken and cook for about 8–10 minutes each side until done. You can heat up any remaining marinade in a small pan sitting on the grill and then pour over the chicken before serving. If the chicken is still pink inside, pop it back on the grill for another couple of minutes or so.

Veggie sticks

Grilling vegetables really brings out the true flavours so vegetable kebabs are not only healthy but also delicious. They can be a meal in themselves although you can always add meat if you wish. You should use onions, mushrooms, peppers, courgettes and then whatever else you can buy locally.

Preparation and cooking time: 20–25 minutes

Ingredients (serves four):
4 tablespoons olive oil
2 tablespoons red wine vinegar
2 tablespoons lemon juice
1 tablespoon English mustard
1 tablespoon chopped fresh parsley
1 tablespoon chopped fresh basil
2 cloves of garlic, crushed
Black pepper
8 button mushrooms
4 medium sized onions
2 courgettes
1 large green pepper
1 large red pepper
1 large aubergine (if available)

In a large plastic bag, mix all the non-vegetable ingredients thoroughly and then add the vegetables and toss. The longer you marinate the vegetables the better they will taste but if it is a hot day, it is safer to start cooking them after 30–40 minutes.

Warm the grill and alternate the vegetables on skewers. Place the skewers on the grill and cook for about 10–15 minutes, adding more marinade as needed. Delicious.

right: Let your imagination run riot when it comes to campfire cooking. You will be amazed at what you can achieve – and so will your family and friends as they tuck in.

DELICIOUS DESSERTS

Instant lemon curd

Preparation and cooking time: 10–15 minutes

Ingredients (serves four):
100g (3½oz) caster sugar
1 egg
3 tablespoons fresh lemon juice
1 teaspoon grated lemon zest
4 tablespoons unsalted butter

Mix all the ingredients together in a pan, bring to the boil and when it starts to thicken, remove from the heat and allow to cool. Spread it on a slice of fruit cake, a piece of gingerbread or a warm scone.

above: Camping on the banks of the river Thames at Sunbury, 1897.

Chocolate delight

This is not a dessert for those on a diet, but never mind – you are on holiday.

Preparation and cooking time: 10 minutes

Ingredients (serves four):
100g (3½oz) caster sugar
50g (1¾oz) unsweetened cocoa powder
40g (1¼oz) plain flour
480ml (16fl oz) milk
2 eggs, yolks only
170g (6oz) chocolate chips
1 teaspoon vanilla extract
1 tablespoon butter
115g (4oz) raspberries, blackberries or strawberries (or a mixture)

In a pan mix together the sugar, cocoa and flour and then slowly add the milk, stirring all the time. Cook over a low heat until the mixture starts to bubble gently (it must not bubble too vigorously). Reduce the heat and simmer for another 2 minutes.

Remove from heat, pour half the mixture into a bowl, beat in the 2 egg yolks until blended and return it to the pan.

Add the chocolate chips and bring to a gentle boil and then simmer for 2 minutes, stirring frequently. Add the vanilla and butter, simmer for another minute, still stirring, then remove from heat and allow to cool.

If you are preparing this in the evening it may be cool enough for the dessert to sit out while it cools. If it is warm, transfer the mixture into a container and keep it in the cooler.

You can serve in dishes with a liberal helping of berries on top or, if you are having strawberries, leave the hulls (top leaves) on so that you can use them to dunk the strawberries into the chocolate.

Apple crunch

Preparation and cooking time: 30 minutes

Ingredients (serves four):
4 large apples, cored, peeled and sliced
90g (3oz) brown sugar
100g (3½oz) plain flour
45g (1½oz) instant porridge oats
115g (4oz) butter, softened

Layer the apples in the bottom of an ovenproof dish. In a bowl, mix together the sugar, flour and oats and then blend in the butter. Spread the mixture over the apples and cook for about 30 minutes. Check every now and then to make sure the bottom layers of fruit are not getting burned.

Summer fruit pudding

Preparation time: 10 minutes

Ingredients (serves four):
Several digestive biscuits
230g (8oz) cream cheese
230g (8oz) whipped cream
115g (4oz) raspberries
115g (4oz) blackberries
115g (4oz) blackcurrants

Line the bottom of a bowl with crumbled digestive biscuits or similar (chocolate digestives are very good.) Mix the cream cheese and whipped cream together until blended. Add the fruit and layer on top of the biscuits. Instant pudding!

left: Greengrocer's paper bag, 1970, urging customers to buy English fruit.

right: Collecting fallen apples in the orchards at Killerton, Devon. They are used to make the excellent cider and chutney sold in the National Trust shop there.

SECTION THREE:

GAMES AND ADVENTURES

EXPLORING THE COUNTRYSIDE

As you walk in the countryside, take in your surroundings and try to interpret what you see. The footpath you are on may have been followed by others for hundreds of years; the hill ahead of you could have had an ancient fort on top.

It's also fun to try to figure out the names of places – how do you think Pratts Bottom got its name? It was originally called Spratts Bottom and bottom usually means a valley at the foot of a hill so the assumption is that this valley was owned by someone called Spratt or Pratt. Names of villages and landscape features also tell us a lot about the history of the area – whether they were named by the Romans, Celts, Anglo-Saxons, Vikings, Normans and so on.

Most names are a combination of two or more words. It could be the landowner's name and a feature of the land or the use it was put to – Grimsby means Grim's farm as 'by' is one of the Norse words for farm. Cambridge and Tonbridge derive from the bridge over the rivers Cam and Ton. 'Caster', 'cester' and 'chester' are Anglo-Saxon variations of the Roman word 'castrum' for a camp or fort so that gives us Doncaster (the fort on the River Don), Colchester and so on. Another word used for a fort was 'bury' and that give us place names ending in 'bury' or 'borough'.

Words ending in 'den' or 'coombe' denote a valley while those ending in 'don' normally indicate a hill. Place names ending in 'wich', 'ton', 'ham', 'thorpe' and 'stock' derive from a farm or settlement founded there. 'Hurst' is a wooded hill, while names ending in 'ly', 'ley' or 'leigh' signify a clearing in the wood. Hundreds of years ago most of the country was forested and the names of the most common trees in an area became part of the name of the village – Sevenoaks in Kent and Poplar in London are good examples.

Many words in Cornwall start with the word 'pen', which means a headland, such as Penzance, while names ending in 'stow' or 'stowe' generally indicate an ancient meeting place.

If you are out walking and heading towards a village, try to figure out how it got its name. Can you spot any features in the landscape that will give you a clue?

above: The countryside is an ever changing palette of colour from season to season. This particularly magnificent autumnal view was taken on the Ashridge Estate, Hertfordshire. Running along the main ridge of the Chilterns, the area supports a rich variety of wildlife.

Apart from the place names that can tell you a lot about the history of the area, try to learn more about the local folklore. Every part of Britain is steeped in a rich folk heritage – from ghosts and magical places to centuries' old customs, festivities and traditions.

The western half of the country including Wales and the South West is steeped in mysticism. It was home to the Druids and the Celts, Stonehenge and ancient temples such as Avebury, which predates the famous ring of stones on Salisbury Plain.

Learning more about this folklore adds immeasurably to your enjoyment of the area – and provides some great spooky stories round the campfire.

Loch Ness is famous for Nessie but many bodies of water throughout the UK have their own legends about strange beasts. There are claims that a giant eel-like creature has been spotted in Windermere on several occasions over the last few decades. While

above: An aerial view of the White Horse of Uffington, an ancient figure carved into the chalk downs of Oxfordshire.

water monsters take refuge in the lakes, dragons are said to have roamed several parts of the country, especially in the South West.

There are many legends of mermaids being sighted offshore, especially around the Cornish coast, while all round the coast, ghost ships are said to sail over the sandbanks on which they foundered hundreds of years ago. There are stories of coastal caves used by pirates and of treasures still unfound.

In many parts of Britain there are hills said to be frequented by fairies while others are home to witches. Wherever there are huge boulders, there are often stories about the giants who threw them there, angry at something or other.

Other strange sights in many parts of the country are chalk figures carved on hillsides. The White Horse, near Uffington in Berkshire, is one of the best examples and was carved more than 2,000 years ago although what it represents is debatable. Other carvings include the Long Man at Wilmington in East Sussex and Dorset's Cerne Abbas giant.

Folklore also abounds about bridges. Many are said to be controlled by fairies or the Devil while ogres live beneath others. Crossroads are also the stuff of legends and often associated with evil and death – not surprisingly because many criminals were hanged and left there so that they could be seen by everyone passing by.

Village churchyards are also a great place to learn more about a local area and tombstones can yield a wealth of information. Many of the inscriptions are also amusing. For instance, I like the inscription on a tombstone in Kingsbridge, Devon, which reads:

Here lie I at the chancel door,
Here lie I because I'm poor,
The farther in the more you pay,
Here lie I as warm as they.

If the church is near the coast, you will often see the graves of seamen who died at sea during storms, while everywhere you can get an impression of how tough life must have been two or three centuries ago because of the comparatively young ages of the deceased and the large number of children who died at an early age.

Many churches were built on top of hills because they doubled as fortified places of refuge as well and you can still see the tall slits in towers through which villagers fired their arrows at attackers.

above: 1930s postcard showing the haunts of the Loch Ness Monster.

The buildings of Britain are fascinating to study. Centuries-old thatched cottages that we often take too much for granted are always a source of great awe to foreign visitors. As you travel around the country you can learn so much by studying the buildings, not just the architectural style but often the history and culture of the area as well – from the magnificent stately homes set in vast, landscaped estates to the tiny farm cottages and from the grandiose city centre municipal buildings to the imposing fortresses and castles.

For almost 2,000 years buildings around Britain were constructed from materials that were available locally. It was impractical to bring in materials as in most cases there were no roads or methods of transport. That is why many old buildings that survive in Yorkshire down to Dorset are made from limestone, while granite is popular in Wales and Cornwall. Timber was, of course, the most popular building material as almost the whole country was forested up until 300

below: You never know what you might find when you take a hike in the countryside. It could be ruins of an old mine, a prehistoric fort or a wind pump – like this one at Wicken Fen in Cambridgeshire.

years ago, but timber structures often didn't survive because of fire and the damp British climate. Fortunately some excellent examples of old wooden buildings still exist, such as the 16th-century Link Farm in Egerton, Kent and the magnificent Lower Brockhampton Hall in Herefordshire, which dates back to the 14th century and was bequeathed to the National Trust in 1946.

Bricks, brought back as ballast from the Low Countries, became fashionable in the Middle Ages. The Manor Farm, near St Neots in Cambridgeshire, is an outstanding example of a Tudor brick manor house, for example.

Then, of course, you have all the magnificent religious buildings – from old abbeys to Gothic cathedrals. There are industrial buildings – old mills and potteries, copper, tin and coalmines and lighthouses.

above: Towanwroath Shaft engine house, now ruinous but once housing a Cornish beam engine used to pump water from Wheal Coates mine on the cliffs near St Agnes, Cornwall.

In the Peak District National Park, almost everywhere you look there are industrial archaeological and historical remains dating back to the Bronze Age – and the magnificent scenery as well. And, of course, this is repeated all around the country from the ancient tin mines of Cornwall to windmills in East Anglia and ancient ironworks in Kent and Sussex. Britain has a wonderful heritage to protect and enjoy.

By studying the buildings and historical remains you can often tell how prosperous an area was and how the local people were employed. Make it a game to see who can discover the oldest building while you are on a trip. Then take a photograph and see what more you can learn about it when you get home.

BASIC NATURE SKILLS

I t may seem a little obvious but nature is all round you. How often do you take notice of it? As you are walking down a trail, how many of the tree species can you recognise? Can you name the bird that you can hear singing but is hidden in a clump of bushes? Do you know the names of the various wild flowers or that strange-looking fungus?

After a night of rain can you identify which animal made the tracks crossing the path or know from the marks which bird hopped through the mud? If you really want to marvel at the complexity of nature, watch a column of ants going about their business – but not, hopefully, inside your tent. When you find a column you will notice some are going one way and the rest are going in the opposite direction. It's a bit like the many lanes of a busy motorway. Follow the ants one way to see where they are going – it is likely to be a food source – and then follow them back to find out where the nest is.

The best way to observe wildlife is to be up and about when they are. For daytime animals and birds that usually means early morning and late afternoon until dusk and for nocturnal creatures, like badgers, foxes and owls, that means getting up in the middle of the night.

above right: There are hundreds of species of fungi in the UK, which play a vital part in woodland habitats, like these on the Holnicote Estate in Somerset.

below right: Being able to identify the things you see in nature enhances the countryside experience – like this adult male green woodpecker about to enter its nest.

You also need quite a lot of patience. If you are walking along a path you might be lucky enough to spot something but the chances are that the creature will hear you first and be off long before you get the chance to see it. Find a good vantage point, overlooking a lake or a clearing in a wood, sit down and wait quietly – let the animals and birds come to you.

A good pair of binoculars will allow you to examine them in much more detail and a field guide will help you identify things you have not seen before. It is also a good idea to have a notebook and pen so you can make notes about your observations. You can even get waterproof notebooks and pens so that you can write in any weather conditions. You don't have to be a good artist to make field notes. If you are watching an unknown bird, make a sketch of its silhouette, estimate its size in relation to other birds such as a sparrow or thrush,

DID YOU KNOW?

Bird feathers are made from keratin, the same material that your fingernails and toenails are made of. As fingernails grow and need cutting, bird feathers become worn, which is why birds moult, shedding their old feathers and growing new ones.

above: When you are walking through woodland, such as this one at Alderly Edge in Cheshire, see how many different trees, plants, birds and animals you can spot. If you don't recognize something, makes notes, take a photo and look it up back at camp.

and note any identifiable features or behaviour patterns. For instance, the bird may have a distinct yellow eye stripe or sit on a fence bobbing its tail up and down, a long tail or a short tail, a thick bill or a curved bill. All these observations will help you identify it later on. Once you have been able to identify it that is not the end of the story. The next time you observe it you will notice many other things about it, how it flies, feeding patterns, mating habits, different calls and so on. Learning about nature is a never-ending project.

You can take all this knowledge back with you because you don't only observe wildlife in the country. You could be sitting at home in a town when you hear a bird calling as it flies overhead – and have the satisfaction of knowing what it is.

If you are near the coast, spend a few hours sitting on top of a cliff looking out at sea. In many parts of the country you can spot seals, dolphins and porpoises. There are also huge bird colonies along the coastline where you might watch gulls, terns, skuas, puffins, guillemots and many other species.

You will often see feathers on the ground, so take them back to the camp and try to identify which bird they came from. Try to determine if they are tail or wing feathers, and whether they are from an immature or an adult bird.

As you walk along, turn over rocks every now and again to see what you can find underneath. There are whole cities of insects living below in the dark. You might even find some lizards, a slow worm or a smooth snake. Always put the rock back as you found it.

Nature watching is a year-round activity. There may be more to see in the warmer months but in the autumn when the leaves start to fall, you can see abandoned nests in trees and hedgerows. Can you identify what bird made the nest or could it be a squirrel's dray? Can you identify any of the leaves on the ground? Do you know what tree they came from? There are fallen nuts to identify – and, if they are safe, to eat. In the winter when the snow is on the ground, it is much easier to spot tracks and follow them.

The more you know about nature, the more you will marvel at it and the greater will be your satisfaction as a result. Even better, you will be able to pass this knowledge on to your children.

There are lots of great field guides to choose from covering the entire animal and plant kingdoms. Check out your local library to see what you like and then order copies from your bookshop.

right: You never know what you might spot while out walking. This male viviparous lizard lives further north than any other lizard species.

far right: The red squirrel, rare in many parts of the country, has been a native for several thousand years while the grey squirrel, imported from North America in 1876, is now the most common.

WEATHER FORECASTING – THE COUNTRY WAY

With mobile phones, pocket radios and GPS devices it is easy to keep in touch with the latest weather forecasts and that is important if you are out in the countryside – especially in more remote areas. Knowing what the weather is likely to do can allow you to descend to lower ground for safety if you are in the hills or return to your campsite to the cover of your tent. It can also help you plan the day's events to get the most out of your trip. For instance, if it is likely to rain all day it is much better to plan a visit to somewhere sheltered than to go for a long, wet hike in the hills.

However, well before all these hi-tech communication gadgets were available, country folks were able to predict – reasonably accurately – what the weather was going to do from seeing what was going on around them, and their observations still hold true today.

If you are camping in a country site, find a large pine cone and keep it near the tent. An open cone indicates dry weather, but if it closes up, it is probably going to rain. If you are near the coast, seaweed can also be a good weather forecaster. If the seaweed feels dry to the touch the weather is likely to be dry; if the seaweed feels moist, it is going to be wet. The scientific explanation for this is that the seaweed reacts to changes in humidity so low humidity indicates dry weather and vice versa.

A red sky at night, a mist at dawn or heavy early morning dew

left: The marsh marigold is one of the oldest British plants and fossils show that it was around before the Ice Age. Perhaps that is why they are so good at predicting the weather.

above: A walker admires the striking red sky sunset at Wasdale Head, Cumbria. The weather following a sunset like this is likely to be fine.

all predict a warm day ahead. When cows are sitting or bunched together in the corner of a field it means rain is on its way. Also, cows don't like rain on their faces so if they are all sitting down and facing the same way, the rain is probably going to come from the other direction. Bees also dislike rain and so a stream of bees heading back to their hives is a sure sign of impending wet weather. Another good rule of thumb is 'Rain before seven, fine before eleven'.

Bats are usually silent when they fly so when they squeak on the wing this indicates that it is likely to rain quite soon. Gnats bite more if wet weather is on its way – although that is little consolation and a bug spray is still a good idea. Gnats also like to swarm in the open if the weather is fine but if rain threatens they stay in the shade.

In scores of ways, animals, birds and flowers can help us predict the weather and tell us whether we will need our waterproofs. Wild marigolds open very wide if the day is set to be fine but don't open at all if rain is imminent. The scarlet pimpernel closes its small red flowers when it senses approaching rain, as do dandelions and daisies. When the flowers open again you know it is set to be fair for some time.

Swallows soar high in the sky hunting for insects in fine weather but fly much lower if the weather is changing and rain is coming. Geese fly high if it going to be fine but low when a storm is coming. Many songbirds also warn of approaching wet weather. Blackbirds, robins and thrushes sing from the tops of the trees when it is going to stay fine, but sing from the lower branches if it is going to rain.

Spiders sense the approach of stormy weather and rush about spinning extra strands to hold their web in place. That is the time you check your tent guy lines and make sure everything is secure.

Several species of tree – such as sycamore, poplar and lime – are also great predictors of wet weather. Many turn their leaves so that the lighter undersides are visible. The scientific reason for this is that as the moisture content in the atmosphere increases, the leaf stalks become moist and twist, turning the leaf over.

above: Rooks are incredible weather barometers. By watching their flight you can tell if it is going to be fine or wet, calm or windy – and you can plan accordingly.

When rooks leave their nests at dawn and fly off in a straight line, the day will be fine. When they leave later and take a zigzag course, it is going to be wet and if they stay at home, strong winds are likely.

below: During the summer, lime trees like these ones at Winkworth Arboretum in Surrey, expose the lighter underside of their leaves if it is going to rain – warning you that it is time to get out the waterproofs.

The clouds can also help us make accurate weather forecasts. A mackerel sky means that any rain will be light and quickly over. Thin and wispy cirrus clouds are a sign of fair weather. Altocumulus clouds in the summer warn of approaching thunderstorms while nimbostratus clouds will bring rain.

As you sit round the campfire look up into the night sky and find out what the weather has in store for you the next day. A watery moon indicates approaching rain, while a clear moon means a fine day ahead, although in winter this could also mean a frost. Even the colour of the moon tells us something – a pale moon means it is going to rain, a red moon is forecasting winds and a white moon tells us that the day ahead will be dry.

Always pay attention to what the animals and birds are doing, especially if you are out walking in more remote areas. Deer and Highland cattle will make their way down to lower ground if they sense incoming bad weather so, if you are hiking in the hills, follow their example and head back to your campsite.

right (from top): Mackerel sky, cirrus clouds, altocumulus clouds and nimbostratus clouds. By identifying different cloud formations you can predict the weather.

GAMES AND ACTIVITIES

KNOTTY PROBLEMS

Learning how to tie knots is a fun game but it can be a skill that is really worth having if you are camping. It will come in useful if you are building a woodland den (see page 158) or constructing a kite (see page 168) and knowing how to tie a knot that you can untie easily will save you lots of knotty problems in the future. If you like climbing, caving or potholing, knowing how to tie the right knots is essential.

If you want to learn the ropes, literally, sit in a group around the campfire and practise tying the two ends of a piece of rope together. Man has been tying knots since Prehistoric times and today there are hundreds of different knots that can be used for a wide range of purposes. There are even decorative knots that can be fun to make and are incredibly elaborate.

The four most useful knots are the reef, bowline, sheet bend and the clove hitch, and each are suitable for a particular purpose.

Never tie a knot if the ends of the rope are frayed and remember that when you tie two pieces of rope together you also weaken the overall strength – the weakest point is almost always the knot.

Bukta solves your knotty problems

"It can't be done" is a phrase unknown in Bukta's vocabulary. Any problem which concerns Scout Clothing and Equipment can be settled (with the least possible call upon your pocket) by consulting the Bukta catalogue "Scoutannica."

Everything marked "Bukta" is of outstanding merit and is designed to fill a specific purpose in Scouting.

SCOUTANNICA 1932 EDITION is the Bukta Catalogue which helps you to better scouting and camping. Every Scout should have one, and if you have not yet obtained yours get one from your local Outfitter, or write to Dept. I. 21, E. R. Buck & Sons, Ltd., Campedia House, Whitworth Street, Manchester. (Wholesale only.)

KESTREL AND FALCON

MARTIN AND SWALLOW

WANDERLUST HIKE TENT

One of Bukta's greatest successes is the wonderful range of **TENTS** for all purposes. Here are three styles—there are many more, for all purposes, at prices from **13/11**

Bukta Regd.

SCOUT CLOTHING & EQUIPMENT

above: 1932 advertisement for Bukta, publisher of the *Scoutannica* catalogue featuring all conceivable clothing and equipment needed to be a fully fledged boy scout including tents and ropes for knotting.

Reef knot

The reef knot, also called a square knot, is a good knot to start with because it is easy to learn and very practical. It can be used to fasten two pieces of rope together securely and has the advantage that it can easily be undone. It has been in use for centuries and when the Greeks tied it, it was known as the Hercules because it was so strong. Remember: left over right and right over left is the way to tie the knot.

1   Take one end of rope in your left hand and the other in your right hand.
2   Take the rope in your left hand and cross it over and then behind the rope in your right hand. Bring it back up in front.
3   Take the rope now in your right hand and cross it over and behind the rope in your left hand, then thread it through the loop and pull it.
4   As you pull the rope the knot will tighten.
5   To undo just push the two loops apart.

Sheet bend

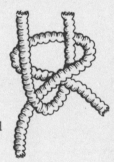

The sheet bend knot is used to tie two pieces of rope together. It gets its name because it is used to tie sail ropes, and these ropes are called sheets. The advantage of this knot, other than it is easy and fast to do, is that it can be safely used to join ropes of different diameters.

1   Take the end of the thicker piece of rope in your left hand and bend it back on itself to form an eye. Hold this eye firmly in your left hand.
2   With your right hand, insert the end of the other thinner rope into the eye from behind.
3   Pull it through and wrap the rope around the eye so that the end tucks back under itself on top of the eye. Pull the standing parts of the ropes to tighten the knot.

Clove hitch

The clove hitch is used to go round an object so is often used to moor boats. It is also a great knot to secure your tent poles.

1   Place one the end of the rope around a pole or tree to form a loop.
2   Continue around, making a second loop above the first until the ropes cross.
3   Tuck the end of the rope under the second loop at the cross and pull to tighten.

Bowline

A bowline allows you to make a loop at one end of the rope. The loop is usually temporary but the knot is strong enough that it can be permanent. It is probably the most widely used knot by sailors all over the world. It does not slip and is easy to untie even when under strain. You slip the other end of the rope through the loop to secure an object securely. Once you get really good at knots, you can tie a bowline with one hand!

One way to remember how to tie a bowline is to think about a rabbit and its rabbit hole. The rabbit comes out of its hole, runs round the tree and hops back down the hole again.

1   First make the 'hole' – a loop about 15cm (6in) from one end of the rope, crossing the short end over the longer one. The short end of rope that is left is called the 'bitter' end. The other end of the rope is the standing end.
2   Holding the loop with the fingers of one hand, tuck the bitter end through the loop, then up and behind the standing end (the tree) and then bring it round and back through the loop (this is the rabbit coming out of its hole, going round the tree and hopping back down the hole again).
3   Hold the rope in one hand and the two pieces that form the loop in the other and pull to tighten the knot.

BUILDING A WOODLAND DEN

Building your own den in the woods is fun and there are usually loads of natural building materials to work with. It is a great way to learn more about nature and the countryside and many organisations, including the Forestry Commission and the National Trust, offer den-building classes for these reasons. Another reason for learning how to build a den is that it is a great survival skill. If you were ever to be stranded in a remote area without a shelter, being able to build a den in order to stay dry and warm could save your life.

There are, of course, a few ground rules. You should only build a den on public ground where you are allowed access. You should only use natural materials on the ground – fallen branches, leaves, bracken and so on. Never light a fire inside a den and you must be careful to build it in such a way as to minimise any risk of it collapsing.

After you have finished with it, collect any litter and dismantle your den, scattering the materials around in as natural a way as possible. Of course, if you are building the den in an area close to your home you can keep it up for as long as you like.

Choosing the right spot for the den is important. Never build in a hollow because if it rains you will find yourself sheltering inside a large puddle. Always choose flat or slightly sloping dry ground. Also, avoid dense canopies of branches and leaves overhead as these will continue to drip water on you a long time after any rain has stopped.

Don't build your den near a busy road or too close to water to avoid accidents. You also want to make sure the site is in a safe place that won't be disturbed – or disturb – passers by.

right: Making a camp or teepee in the woods is a great family activity and a fantastic way to enjoy the countryside, using natural materials to construct something useful.

A great den maker doesn't need any tools and the use of knives should be well-supervised. Working out how to break a thick fallen branch into two smaller pieces is a good initiative test and an excellent way of learning how to solve problems together.

If you can find a natural feature such as a leaning tree it will serve as solid starting point on which to build. The easiest sort of den to build is like a teepee. You need several long fallen branches that you can set upright at regular intervals around the tree. All the tops of the branches will meet and you will need some rope or twine to tie them securely together.

You then gather smaller twigs and weave these in and out of the uprights to make a lattice. This is then covered with a thick layer of leaves, ferns and bracken. If you start at the bottom and work upwards you always have an ascending base to build on. Check from inside the den during this process to make sure you cannot see any daylight because if you can you are going to get wet if it rains. Ensure your den is waterproof by adding multiple overlapping

below: When foraging for wood for a den you may come across uprooted tree stumps. Victorian gardeners excavated tree roots and stumps and set them upside down in banks of earth as a type of garden called a Stumpery, as here at the National Trust's Biddulph Grange in Staffordshire.

layers of leaves and other vegetation. This not only stops the water soaking through but also makes it very snug inside.

Check the inside of the den to make sure the floor has no sharp stones. You can add a carpet of more leaves and bracken to make it more comfortable to sit on.

Another sort of den is the tree house. You have to find a tree with spreading limbs that will support the base of your den. You then place branches across the limbs to make a platform and then build up as described above.

If you are building a tree den, however, do not build it high up because you don't want to be injured

above: Early 20th-century illustration of Maid Marian and Robin Hood bow hunting deer in Sherwood Forest, Nottinghamshire.

falling from it. A good rule of thumb is to build the platform no more than 2m (6½ft) above the ground and to make sure that the area below the den is not covered with rocks and other sharp objects so that if you have to jump down you have a soft and safe landing place.

DID YOU KNOW?

According to legend, when Robin Hood was fighting the wicked Sheriff of Nottingham he and his Merry Men lived in Sherwood Forest in dens just like those described above, although theirs were much bigger. Because there was so much poverty in medieval England, thousands of other folks also lived in the woods, building their own shelters and surviving on what they could forage and catch.

WILDLIFE TRACKS

With the exception of flying birds you are more likely to see an animal track than the animal itself – simply because most animals are wary of people and avoid us whenever possible.

The best places to look for tracks are on the beach, the muddy sides of a stream, river or lake, or a trail or footpath, especially after rain when the ground is wet. If you are near water you may find a game trail – a path used by several different animals to get to their watering hole.

If you are lucky you will have a complete set of footprints to examine and use to try to identify the animal that made them. Mostly, however, you will not. Tracks vary enormously and depend on what the animal was doing at the time. If it was fleeing from a predator it would have been running and taking long strides so you may only see partial prints as it scooted over the ground. If the ground is firm, you may not see the animal's toes in the print because it didn't need to grip the ground so tightly for traction.

The fun in tracking is not only to identify the animal but also to try to work out what it was doing at the time – was it being chased, was it looking for prey, was it just out for a stroll or going to get a drink?

left: Rabbits can see behind themselves without turning their head but they have a blind spot right in front of their face.

above: Badger watching is great fun but you have to be patient. Keep your distance and remain quiet and still until the animals emerge. It is well worth the wait.

You can take a photo of the tracks either with your camera or phone or draw a sketch.

It is also fun to make a cast of the track if it is a good one. This is a two-step process. The first process is to make what is called a negative cast. You need a strip of cardboard about 7–8cm (2¾–3in) wide and about 75cm (2½ft) long. Make a circle around the track with the cardboard, pushing it into the surrounding area if possible and closing the circle using a strong paperclip. Next, in a small bowl or beach bucket, mix plaster of Paris and water – about two parts plaster to one part water. You don't want the mixture too thick because it will not pour evenly and will start to dry almost immediately and you will not finish up with a very good cast. If the mixture is too sloppy it will take too long to set. It should have the consistency of pancake batter.

Pour the mixture evenly over the track, covering it completely, until the level is about 2.5cm (1in) below the top of the cardboard. Always pour the plaster from the outside in so that it can run from the surrounding ground into the track. If you pour directly into the track you may destroy some of the features. Then sit back and be patient while the plaster of Paris sets – normally after about 20 minutes or so. When you are sure it is hard, gently slide a knife under one edge and work your way around and under the circle to separate it from any vegetation or dirt; carefully lift it up. Although dry the cast may still be brittle so handle with care. You should not try to remove any other dirt for at least 24 hours until the cast has completely hardened.

Once back at your campsite, you can clean up the negative cast by brushing off any dirt and other debris. Some people like their casts this way and you can paint them as they are. You could go one stage further, however, and make a positive cast that will be an exact replica of the track you saw. Clean up the negative cast and cover it with a thin layer of petroleum jelly. On a clean, flat surface covered with several sheets of newspaper, make another mould using your cardboard strip to form a ring and fill it with plaster of Paris. As it starts to set, press the negative cast gently but firmly into the plaster. The grease should prevent it from sticking. After about 10 seconds very carefully remove the negative cast and let the plaster harden to give you a perfect track replica.

below: Hedgehogs are voracious hunters but until the last century they were hunted themselves by countryfolk who popped them into stews.

above: There are few sights as cute as a baby seal and luckily, there are many sites around the country where you can see them, such as the National Trust's Blakeney National Nature Reserve in Norfolk. They are easy to spot due to the distinctive tracks they leave in wet sand.

CAPTURE THE FLAG GAME

Capture the Flag is a fun game to play, especially in the woods as you have more places to hide although you can play it anywhere. You need two teams and this is a great way to get to know your neighbours at the campsite – invite them to join in because this is a game that is best played with lots of players.

Each team has a flag – it could be a tea towel or a shirt or whatever. Work out an area in which the game is to be played. Imagine it is like a football pitch with two halves – your territory and theirs. You tie your flag in what would be your goal area and this is your base. The other team does the same at their end.

The goal is to capture the other team's flag and get it back to the home base. Once players cross from their home territory into the 'enemy's' territory they can be tagged. There are lots of different rules about tagging. One is that if players are tagged, they are out and must leave the game; another says that the tagged player must join the other side. I prefer the rule that says that the tagged player returns to their home base and starts out again. Once the flag has been captured, the player can pass it on to someone else if they have a better chance of getting it back to base.

It's not just a fun game; it is also a game of strategy. Teams can nominate decoys – people who will try to deliberately draw the other team players to them so that their team mates have a clear run at the flag.

MR WOLF'S DINNER TIME GAME

Nobody is really sure how this game started but it is now played all over the English-speaking world, although in the USA, for some reason, it is known as What Time Is It, Mr Fox?

It is a form of tag with many variations and can be played with as few as three players or as many as you can muster.

One player is selected as Mr Wolf and he or she has to stand at a given distance from the other participants. It could be ten or fifteen steps away, although this largely depends on how much space you have to play in. When Mr Wolf is in position the rest of the players ask 'What's the time, Mr Wolf?' Mr Wolf has two options. He or she can either reply by shouting out a time – say 3 o'clock, in which case all the players take three steps towards Mr Wolf. However, if Mr Wolf calls out 'It's dinner time', he can dart forward and try to tag one of the players as they try to race back to the start line where they are safe. If a tag takes place, that player becomes the new Mr Wolf.

As a variation, you can have a rule that Mr Wolf has to face away from the other players, so Mr Wolf cannot see how close they may be getting. In this case, the first player to tag Mr Wolf is the winner.

below: There are lots of family games you can play in the countryside especially when there are lots of trees to hide behind, like in this orchard at Trerice in Cornwall.

MAKING AND FLYING A KITE

You can make a kite out of odd bits and pieces you find around the campsite. A couple of sticks, a plastic bag, a few strips of newspaper and a ball of string are all you need for the kite, although you will also need a ruler, some tape and a knife.

The most basic form of kite consists of a cross made from two pieces of stick or dowel – one about 60cm (2ft) long and the other about 50cm (20in) long.

1 Make a notch at both ends of each stick – all the notches must run in the same direction.
2 Using a measure or ruler, make a mark on the long stick about 15cm (6in) from one end. Make another mark on the shorter stick at the midway point. Lay the longer stick on the ground with the shorter stick on top, and match up the marks to form the cross, making sure that all the notches are parallel with the ground.
3 You then use string to secure the sticks together firmly, first around where they cross and then following the notches to form a diamond shape all around the kite. Make sure the string is taut.
4 Take a large piece of brown paper or a plastic bag that is larger than the frame and cut out the sail. There should be at least a 5cm (2in) overlap on all sides. Fold the overlap back over the string and tape or glue down.
5 Attach a small strip of tape to the top and bottom of the kite and, using a pencil or similar, punch a hole through the tape.
6 Take a piece of string about 60cm (2ft) long and thread it through the hole in the top of the kite; secure it with a knot and then thread the other end through the hole at the bottom of the kite. This forms the bridle.
7 You attach one end of your ball of string to the bridle about a third of the way along its length from the top. After a few test flights you can adjust this positioning for a better flight..
8 Finally you add the tail, which should be about 2m (6½ft) long. It needs a little weight for flying stability so use ribbon or strips of paper to make bows along its length.

above: Front cover of *The Scout* magazine, 1932. Organisations like the Scouts and Guides have pioneered teaching countryside and outdoor skills such as kite flying and camping.

GAMES AND ADVENTURES 169

All you need now is a nice open space – and lots of wind!
Flying a kite is really a two-person job: one to hold the kite
in the air and the other to control the tethering string. At a given signal,
the person holding the kite should let it go while the person with the string
should give a sharp jerk to give it lift. You don't need to unwind a lot of
string because the secret is to release the kite and let the wind lift it into the
air. Because the kite is so light it is usually quite easy to get lift-off but then
you need velocity to keep it up and gain altitude and this involves charging
down the beach or wherever, slowly letting more string out as you go. It's
not only fun but a great way to get fit as well!

You could have a family competition to see who can make the
best-looking kite and the most aerodynamic.

above: You can fly kites almost anywhere where there is clear ground but beaches, cliffs and hilly areas are
best – like the North Downs in Surrey – because of the onshore breezes and thermals.

DODGE BALL

The game, as the name suggests, is all about dodging the ball. You normally have two teams with the same number of players, but you can just have a general free-for-all if you like when it is every player for themselves.

You can also play with as many balls as you like, although the game can get very hectic. Start off by using three balls, which will keep you on your toes. Mark out a playing area with two halves. Each team must stay in their half. The aim is to throw the ball so that it hits a player on the other side without bouncing off the floor. If the ball hits the player that player is out and must leave the playing area for two minutes (or whatever time limit you impose), after which they can return. If the player catches the ball without it striking their body they can throw it back at the other team. Even with three balls in play you have to keep your wits about you. The winning team is the one that manages to eliminate all the players on the other side.

There are, of course, many variations of the game. You can have a row of skittles – three or five – at each end of your playing area. Teams now have to throw at players on the other side and try to knock down the skittles. If a skittle is knocked down it stays down and the game ends as soon as all the skittles have been knocked down or all the players eliminated.

If you decide not to have teams and go for the free-for-all option, you still need some rules. Players with the ball must throw it where they are; they are not allowed to move with it. Once they have thrown the ball and it falls to the ground another player can go and retrieve it but must then throw from that spot. Players without a ball are free to run around to avoid being hit. It is best to play with only one or two balls. This can be a very exciting game and there is no limit on how many people can play.

Because you are throwing the ball at people, it is obviously a good idea to use balls that are made of soft materials. If you are playing on the beach, remember that wet balls can hurt.

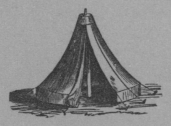

ROUNDERS

Rounders dates back to Tudor times and Henry VIII is reputed to have played it at Hampton Court. It can be played on any open area and you can adapt the rules depending on how many people are playing. According to the rules there should be two teams of nine players. Teams alternate between batting and fielding. The batter has to hit a ball thrown underarm by the bowler and while it is in play, either in the air or moving on the ground, run to the first of four bases. If the ball thrown by the bowler is too wide it is a no-ball and the batter can decide whether it is safe to run or not. If the batter hits a no-ball and is caught it doesn't count. A batter can't run to first base if it is already 'loaded' (if another batter is already there) and that applies to all the bases. So if any of the bases are loaded when a new batter takes over, the onus is on those already on a base to get to the next one so that everyone can keep moving round. Each base is also guarded by one of the fielding team. If a runner tries to get to the next base and the ball is thrown and caught by the person guarding that base, the runner is out. Normally batters are allowed three good balls each and if they fail to hit any of them and are not able to run to first base, they are out. The next batter than has a turn and so on until everyone on the team has been to bat. The teams then change roles – with the batting team now fielding and vice versa.

A big difference between rounders and baseball is that in baseball the batter normally drops the bat after a hit as he runs to first base. In rounders you have to keep hold of your bat and you are out if you drop it.

The batter is allowed to run round all the bases if he can and if the batter does so, it is a home run and the team is awarded one point. The team with the most points at the end of the game wins. A game normally consists of five or seven innings but extra innings can be added to break a tie.

The chances are that you won't be able to muster nine players every time, but as long as both teams have the same number of players that is fine. There are normally four bases but you can make do with three or even two if you are playing with small children. There are also special beach rounders sets that you can buy with plastic bat and ball, which are safer. The plastic bat does not allow you to hit the ball so far, which means you are not likely to disturb other people on the beach and if you are hit by the ball it won't hurt as much.

left: A small but determined member of a Boys Club lines up to bat alongside their tents. Boys clubs were founded in 1925 as a network of voluntary youth clubs across Britain.

MIDNIGHT HIKES

There are two sorts of midnight hike. The first can be a fun adventure of just walking in the dark (with torches – head torches are best) to experience what it is like. It is quite interesting to walk a trail during the daytime, noting as many features along it as you can and then repeat the walk at night. Everything looks different. You will not be able to find many of the features you saw during the day and it is very easy to get disorientated and lose direction.

The other sort of midnight hike – my favourite – is to go out in the dark to see how many creatures you can spot. Most animals and birds get up at dawn to feed, rest up during the day, especially if it is hot, feed again before dusk and then retire for the night. That is why, when you go for a walk in the early afternoon there are far fewer birds around and almost no animals. However, at night nocturnal animals and birds come out to eat and play, and providing you are quiet and stay still, you can have a grandstand view as they go about their nightly business.

You may see bats zooming around looking for insects. You may see an owl gliding through the trees or over a meadow looking for a meal. Owls have special feathers, especially on their wings, which allow them to fly silently, enabling them to be such successful predators. Their prey doesn't hear them coming until it is too late.

There are many birds that sing at night – including nightjars and nightingales, reed and sedge warblers and corncrakes. Most are migratory so you will only hear them in the summer or autumn months. Many redwings and fieldfares are autumn visitors from Scandinavia and they sing between feeding. They not only feed at night but they also migrate at night, navigating by the stars.

left: Front cover of *The Hiker and Camper*, August 1933, the 1930s magazine devoted to outdoor pursuits.

right: Owls have feathers with serrated edges which makes them almost silent in flight. So if you are out for a midnight hike the first you see of an owl might be when it swoops over your head.

AUGUST   1933   VOL. 3. No. 7

THE HIKER & CAMPER

6^D

THE ALL THE YEAR ROUND MAGAZINE FOR EVERYONE WHO LOVES THE OPEN

A Three-Day Hike in Kent	The Unknown Nor'-West Passage to the Lakes
What Austria Offers the Hiker	Canoe Hiking
A Sherwood Forest Hike	Special Caravan Routes

If you go on a midnight hike, it is a good idea to find a clearing and then set up a torch in the middle of it. If you all then move back several steps and sit down you will soon see an array of insects, moths and nocturnal butterflies attracted to the light.

If you are really lucky you might see a badger or a fox. The best way to see a badger is to go out exploring during the day to discover where it lives. Badgers live in a sett – a warren of tunnels, which can have many entrances and escape exits. A large family of badgers can have up to 50 members, although usually it is a lot less. Once you have found out where they live, you can return at night to observe them from a safe distance. It is a good idea to have bushes or trees behind you to help you blend into the background. It is also important to be downwind of the sett so the badgers don't get a whiff of you. Their eyesight is not very good but their sense of smell and hearing more than make up for this.

While you can see deer during the day, they are active at night. The native red deer is the largest species in the UK but you might also see the native roe deer, and the introduced fallow, sika, muntjac and Chinese water deer.

below: The red deer seen here are the largest of the six species found in the UK. Only the red and roe deer are truly native, the other species – fallow, Sika, Muntjac and Chinese water deer – were all imported.

If you are near waterways, be on the lookout for otters, which feed at night. Although they like to play they are still ferocious hunters and as agile on land as they are on water.

Being out at night is great fun, but some basic precautions are needed. Always have a responsible person in charge. Stick to public rights of way. Everyone should have a torch with new batteries and wear stout footwear because it is a lot easier to trip or stub your toes in the dark. Have warm clothing because it can get chilly and take a waterproof if there is a chance of rain. Keep the waterproof in a daypack, though, because if you carry it, it will rustle and that will scare off the animals.

Finally, be alert at all times. Stags start rutting in the autumn, gathering up a harem of females (hinds) prior to mating. The stags become fiercely

above: The best way to learn about nature is to get out and explore, especially if you go out with an expert. Clubs are a great way to take part in activities which are fun and educational.

territorial and will fight off anything invading it – whether it is another deer or a human. You also never know what you might meet in the dark. While it is highly unlikely that you will ever see a wild boar, they are making a comeback in the countryside. They are all escapees from pig farms and are now established throughout southern England and the Forest of Dean with sightings coming in from many other parts of the country. The record for a wild boar is 240kg (37½ stone) but it is the females with a young litter that can be the most dangerous.

Keep a nature diary of walks such as these. Describe the area that you visited, the weather conditions and all the animals, birds and insects that you saw as well as any unusual behaviours that you observed.

POND DIPPING

Hydra, daphnia, stentor and *cyclops* are just a few of the thousands of tiny creatures that you can find in your average country pond. The way to discover them is to pond dip. You use a small net and an old jam jar with a string tied round its neck, which you lower into the water to get your specimens. When using the net, slowly make a figure of eight pattern with it as this will trap more specimens. Don't stir up any sediment and collect your specimens from shaded areas and close to pond vegetation as that it where most pond creatures hang out. The net will trap the larger creatures, such as tadpoles, fish and snails and pieces of plant, and the jar will capture the smaller ones, some of which you can see better with a strong magnifying glass and others that you will only see if you put them on a slide and use a microscope. You need a white plastic bowl – a washing-up bowl is perfect as it allows you to inspect specimens against a light background. You

below: Pond or stream dipping fascinates young and old alike. Fishing for specimens and identifying the catch is a great way to learn about tiny organisms and their behaviours.

should have a tea-strainer or similar, so that you can separate specimens as you pour water out of the jar and a few small containers or plastic bags if you plan to take your finds away and examine them later. You can buy observation jars, which are small containers with a magnified lid. You pop your specimen inside with some clear water and then examine it through the lid – very clever.

above: Frogs are among the wildlife that are commonly spotted when pond dipping.

Like all good naturalists you should also have a notebook and pen to make notes, and a camera to take photos. Wear old clothes because pond dipping can be messy and wear old trainers or wellies.

Ponds hold an enormous array of freshwater organisms from bacteria and protozoa – microscopic single-celled organisms – to algae, worms, snails, frogs, water insects, crustaceans and plants. One of the most widespread pond animals is the mayfly – of which there are over 50 different species in Britain. The most common mayfly is the pond olive, which is unique in that its eggs hatch as soon as they hit the water, although the larvae then spend several months in the pond growing before emerging as adult mayflies.

Caddis flies are relatives of the butterfly but the larvae live under water where they hide in shelters made by pulling the leaves of water plants together and stitching them with strands of silk. Damselflies and dragonflies are the helicopters of the insect world, hovering over ponds before swooping down to catch prey, such as mosquitoes. Like all insects the dragonfly has six legs but it uses them to perch as it can't really walk. They are useful insects to have around

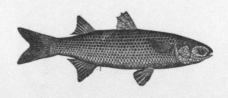

as they have voracious appetites for gnats, mosquitoes and midges.

There are more than 250 species of water beetles, some of which can fly and others can't, and there are water bugs such as the water boatmen, which swim on their backs.

If you are lucky enough to find some frogspawn you can take it back with you and monitor it as it changes first into tadpoles and then into baby frogs – at which point you should release them back into the wild close to a pond or other water source.

above: Watch out for damselflies and dragonflies, such as this spectacular emperor dragonfly.

Ponds also form a special habitat for lots of other creatures that don't live in the water. Dragonflies skim around feeding above the water, wading birds come down to the water's edge to drink and feed, and many animals in the area will use it as their watering hole at night – so look out for animal and bird tracks as well.

Whenever you are playing by water be safe. There should always be adult supervision if young children are involved. Don't go into the water or get too near the edge and never grab on to a branch in order to be able to lean out over the water's edge. If you want to collect water, find a safe place where you can kneel at the edge and collect your water samples without having to stretch. Finally, don't get the water in your mouth – it can carry diseases. It is always a good idea to have a little bottle of hand sanitiser with you and to use it once you have finished collecting and examining your samples.

right: The National Trust runs wildlife identification events such as this one at Oxburgh House in Norfolk. A jar of pond water can contain up to 1,000 different organisms although many are so small that they can't be seen by the human eye.

EXPLORING ROCK POOLS

Tidal rock pools at the beach are great places to find all sorts of strange, tiny creatures. Even a small pool can hold hundreds of different types of creatures and plants – although most will be so small you will not be able to see them without a microscope. However, there will still be many that you can see.

The average rock pool can be home to anemones, urchins, starfish, hermit crabs, small fish, shrimp, seaweed, marine worms, barnacles, mussels and other shellfish, and much more.

As with the Countryside Code, there are some rules that should be followed when exploring rock pools. Cause as little disturbance as possible. If you do lift

below: You could spend hours exploring tidal rock pools, like these at White Park Bay in County Antrim in Northern Ireland. You never know what you are going to find when you look under a rock.

up a rock to see what is underneath, always return it to the same spot, and don't take live creatures away. The other very important rules are: always be aware of the sea and wear footwear. If the tide is out don't get so wrapped up with exploring the rock pool that you don't see it coming in and find yourself trapped. Wear sandals or beach shoes because rocks can be slippery and sharp.

above: Keep an eye out for strange creatures like this headlet anemone when exploring rockpools.

You will need a small net and a beach bucket containing a little sea water in which you can inspect any finds. A magnifying glass is always a good idea so that you can get a really close-up look and a camera is helpful for recording

everything. A good field guide to beaches and beach life will also be useful for identifying what you find.

On your way to and from the rock pool check out the area just above where the waves are coming in to see what shells and other creatures may have been washed in.

Hermit crabs hang out in rock pools and are great fun to watch. Most crabs have armoured plates protecting

above: Shore crabs can be spotted scuttling across beaches and hiding in rock pools.

their body but hermit crabs do not so they take over abandoned shells to live in. When threatened they simply disappear inside the shell where they are safe. As they grow, however, they have to find bigger shells and this has led to a fascinating behavioural pattern. When a large hermit crab inspects an empty shell, it is often surrounded by other hermit crabs who wait in line for the big crab to move into its new home. The next biggest crab then takes over the recently vacated shell and in turn, all the crabs move into a new larger home.

below: This child is rock pool hunting at South Milton Sands in Devon. A net is useful but not necessary if you don't mind swishing your hands around in the water.

MAKING A SUNDIAL AND TELLING THE TIME

There are lots of stories about country folks who always seem to know exactly what time it is. Like the couple who stopped to ask the man sitting on a three-legged stool milking a cow what time it was. He looked up and said 'It's 4 o'clock'. 'That's amazing', the couple said in unison, 'How can you be so sure?' 'Well', said the farmer, 'from where I'm sitting I can just see the clock on the church steeple.'

It may be a silly story but there really are lots of ways of telling the approximate time by observation in the country – not just by looking at church clocks – but by using the sun, the moon and the stars.

If sun up is at 6am in the east and it sets at 6pm in the west it takes twelve hours to travel from east and west. When it is at its highest point in the sky it has got to be halfway there so it is about 12 noon. If the sun is halfway between noon and the western horizon it is around 3pm and so on. If you know that it is noon when the sun is overhead, and either 9am or 3pm when it is halfway to or halfway past its highest point, it is easy to further divide the sun's arc into smaller segments to give you the other hours.

Even though you can't see the sun at night because it is over the horizon you can still use it to tell the time by observing the moon. The moon tells us where the sun is. When there is a full moon, the sun is opposite the moon with the earth in between; when the moon is new, the sun is behind it and the moon is between the sun and earth. When there is a half moon, it is at a right angle to the earth and the sun. If you know where the sun is even though you can't see it and you know that it takes roughly twelve hours to cross the horizon, you should be able to work out its position relative to the east where it will appear at dawn.

The Plough (Big Dipper) and the North Star (Polaris) can also be used to tell the time (see tip on page 187 to find the North Star). If you imagine the North Star is the centre of a clock and you face north, the line from the North Star through the pointers is like the hour hand on a clock. We know that on 7th March in the northern hemisphere this imaginary clock hand would indicate a time of about midnight. For every month after March until August you add one hour and for every month before March back to September you deduct one hour. So if you look at the imaginary clock hand and it seems to be pointing at 2.30am and it is May, you add two hours so the approximate time is 4.30am.

Building a sundial

During the day it is fun to try to guess the right time but one way to check is to build a sundial. The Egyptians and Babylonians used sundials and giant obelisks more than 3,500 years ago to tell the time and by the time of the Greeks and Romans they were extraordinarily accurate.

A sundial consists of an upright rod, called the gnomon, which casts the shadow that tells you the time. You also need a dial plate, which will tell you the hour time depending on where the shadow lands. If you cut out a semi-circular plate the diameter will run from 6am on one side to 6pm on the other. This dial plate can be cut out from paper or card or marked out in the sand if you are at the beach. You could collect seashells or pine cones to mark out the hours as well.

The plate should be divided into hours – from 6am to 6pm – radiating out from the centre point on the baseline. This is also the spot where the gnomon sits upright. The secret, of course, is in positioning the sundial so that it is accurate and that means that the line from the gnomon through the 12 o'clock marker points north. After that you just need some sunshine for an accurate reading!

NAVIGATING BY NATURE

If you don't have a compass you can get a rough approximation of your position from the sun, assuming you can see it. You know the sun rises in the east and sets in the west so at noon it is roughly south, meaning north is the opposite direction.

On a clear night you can locate the seven stars that make up the Plough (or Big Dipper). If you draw a line between the two pointers, the two stars furthest from the handle, and extend this it will lead you to the very bright North Star (Polaris).

One country lore says that moss only grows on the north sides of trees but don't use this as a means of navigation. In areas of high rainfall, moss will grow anywhere.

below: Another idyllic day comes to a close as the moon rises over Bignor Hill on the Slindon Estate in West Sussex.

SECTION FOUR:

CAMPSITES TO VISIT

CAMPSITES TO VISIT

A s mentioned at the beginning of this book, campers in Britain have an enormous choice when it comes to where to go, when to go, what to see and what to do. That choice also extends to where to stay. The following gazetteer lists camping and touring sites located on National Trust land throughout England, Wales and Northern Ireland. Some sites are managed directly by the National Trust, others are leased by the Caravan Club and others are run by National Trust tenant farmers. The sites are in some of the most beautiful areas of the country and you have the added bonus of being able to visit the National Trust properties as well.

For opening times and more information on facilities, charges and any restrictions please contact individual campsites or visit www.nationaltrust.org.uk

SOUTH & SOUTH EAST

Compton Farm
Newport
Isle of Wight PO30 4HF
OS Grid Ref: 196:SZ376851
Tel: 01983 740215
(Adjacent to a farm, which dates back to 1086 and surrounded by an Area of Outstanding Natural Beauty, the campsite nestles in a fold in the Downs and has tremendous views of the chalk cliffs and downland. Within walking distance of the beach at Compton Bay and the coastal footpath)

Etherley Farm
Dorking
Surrey RH5 5PA
OS Grid Ref: 187:TQ139432
Tel: 01306 621423 or 01306 621020
(Small campsite at foot of Leith Hill. The Tower, at 294m (965ft), is the highest point in south-east England. Unlimited tents. Good mountain biking and walking country)

Meadley's Meadow
Ashridge Estate Office
Ringshall
Berkhamsted
Hertfordshire HP4 1LT
OS Grid Ref: 165:SP9713
Tel: 01442 841800 or 01442 842062
Email: ashridge@nationaltrust.org.uk
*(Beautiful site among wonderful and
varied Chilterns countryside. Located
adjacent to the Bridgewater Monument,
visitor centre, tea-room and gift shop on
the Ashridge Estate. Unrestricted access
on foot, with an extensive footpath
network. Trail guides and maps are
available in the shop)*

Oldbury Hill
Holiday Site Manager
Camping and Caravanning Club Site
Styants
Bottom Road
Nr Seal
Sevenoaks
Kent TN15 0ET
OS Grid Ref: 188:TQ577564
Tel: 01732 762728
www.campingandcaravanning
    club.co.uk/oldburyhill
*(Set in 2.4 hectares (6 acres) of quiet and
peaceful countryside surrounded by
woodland walks)*

Slindon
Holiday Site Manager
Camping and Caravanning Club Site
Slindon Park
Arundel
West Sussex BN18 0RG
OS Grid Ref: 197:SU958084
Tel: 01243 814387
www.campingandcaravanning
    club.co.uk
*(Set in an orchard within 1416 hectares
(3,500 acres) of the Slindon Estate,
it is a haven for wildlife and has
beautiful views across the West
Sussex coastal plain)*

Slindon: Gumber Bothy
Bothy Warden
Gumber Farm
Slindon
Arundel
West Sussex BN18 0RN
OS Grid Ref: 197:SU961118
Tel: 01243 814730
*(A sensitively converted traditional
Sussex barn, set in the heart of the Sussex
Downs on a working sheep farm)*

SOUTH WEST

Brownsea Island
Group Bookings
Poole Harbour
Poole
Dorset BH13 7EE
OS Grid Ref: 195:SZ0288
Tel: 01202 492161
Email: brownseaisland@national
    trust.org.uk
*(The Outdoor Centre offers onsite
activities including archery, low ropes,
problem solving, sea kayaking, sailing,
windsurfing and various conservation
and learning activities. All of this while
staying on a 300 hectare (741 acre)
island of heath, coast and woodland,
with unique wildlife and habitats)*

Burrowhayes Farm
West Luccombe
Nr Horner
Porlock
Minehead
Somerset TA24 8HT
OS Grid Ref: 181:SS898460
Tel: 01643 862463
Email: info@burrowhayes.co.uk
www.burrowhayes.co.uk
*(Ideally situated in the glorious Horner
Valley. Superb walks from the site)*

Downhouse Farm
Bridport
Dorset DT6 6AH
OS Grid Ref: 193:SY442918
Tel: 01308 421232
*(On the 800 hectare (1,977 acre) Golden
Cap Estate in a secluded location with
coastal and inland footpaths; within
180m (200yd) of beach)*

Dunscombe Manor Caravan Park
Dunscombe Manor
Salcombe Regis
Sidmouth
Devon EX10 0PN
OS Grid Ref: 192:SY1588
Tel: 01395 513654 or 01395 519038
Email: info@dunscombe-manor.co.uk
www.dunscombe-manor-caravan-
    park.co.uk
*(Situated in 6 hectares (15 acres) of
unspoilt countryside adjacent to the
Heritage Coastal Footpath, Weston
Mouth Beach and the fabulous
Donkey Sanctuary)*

Dyrham Park
Dyrham
Nr Chippenham
South Gloucestershire SN14 8ER
OS Grid Ref: 172:ST743757
Tel: 01179 372501 or 01179 371353
www.nationaltrust.org.uk/dyrhampark
(A late 17th-century house with a
tranquil formal garden and extensive
deer-park, set in 111 hectares (274 acres)
of rolling parkland with spectacular
sweeping views towards Bath and
Bristol)

Higher Penrose Campsite
Penventon Farm
Helston
Cornwall TR13 0RA
OS Grid Ref: SW6325
Tel: 01326 572714 or 07974 186283
(Wonderful walks around Loe Pool and
Bar, Penrose Estate, Porthleven Beach
and the South West Coast Path. Site is
open in July and August)

Highertown Farm
Sal Erskine
Lansallos
Looe
Cornwall PL13 2PX
OS Grid Ref: 200 & 201:SX172517
Tel: 01208 265211
Email: hightertownfarmcampsite@
   nationaltrust.org.uk
(Small campsite situated in the quiet
hamlet of Lansallos with fine views
of the south-east Cornwall coast)

Lundy
The Booking Office
Lundy Shore Office
The Quay
Bideford
Devon EX39 2LY
OS Grid Ref: 180:SS135458
Tel: 01271 863636 or 01237 477779
Email: info@lundyisland.co.uk
www.lundyisland.co.uk
(Unspoilt island, rocky headlands,
outstanding natural beauty, fascinating
history of pirates and smugglers. Famous
for natural history and private postal
service, Marine Nature Reserve.
Excellent base for sea-cliff climbing,
sub-aqua diving in Marine Nature
Reserve, fishing, birdwatching,
nature study)

Prattshayes Farm
The Warden
Maer Lane
Littleham
Exmouth
Devon EX8 5DB
OS Grid Ref: 192:SY0279
Tel: 01395 276626
(Set in a coastal valley near Exmouth with views across the Exe Estuary towards Dartmoor, this small site is close to the South West Coastal Path and the start of the Jurassic Coast)

Southdown Farm
Ringstead
Dorchester
Dorset DT2 8NQ
OS Grid Ref: 194:SY7582
Tel: 01305 852653 or 01305 852788
(One large field 2 mins from sea – the chalk cliffs give fantastic views into Weymouth Bay. Perfectly situated midway between Weymouth and Lulworth on the Dorset Coastal Path, near the tiny hamlet of Ringstead)

St Gabriels
The National Trust West
   Dorset Office
Filcombe Farmhouse
Muddyford Lane
Morcombelake
Dorset DT6 6EP
OS Grid Ref: 193:SY400926
Tel: 01297 561900
(Set within the 800ha (1,977-acre) Golden Cap Estate, this campsite offers unrivalled access to the surrounding countryside. Over 25 miles (40km) of footpaths, 8 miles (13km) of coastline and South West Coast Path, rolling fields and stunning views welcome visitors)

Stourhead
Visitor Reception, Stourhead
Stourton
Warminster
Wiltshire BA12 6QD
OS Grid Ref: 183:ST7735
Tel: 01747 841143 (9am–5pm
   only please)
(Within a short walk of the world-famous 18th-century landscape garden with its enchanting temples, monuments, rare trees and plants set around a magnificent lake)

CENTRAL

Clumber Park Caravan Club Site
The Warden
Limetree Avenue
Clumber Park
Worksop
Nottinghamshire S80 3AE
OS Grid Ref: 120:SK628768
Tel: 01909 484758
www.caravanclub.co.uk
(The 6.8hu (17-acre) site on Hardwick Round is within Clumber Park, which has the longest double lime tree avenue in Europe. Classical bridge over the lake, pleasure gardens)

Ilam Park
The Warden
Ilam Hall Caravan Site
Ashbourne
Derbyshire DE6 2AZ
OS Grid Ref: 119:SK132507
Tel: 01335 350310
Email: ilampark@nationaltrust.org.uk
(Within the South Peak Estate, an area of outstanding beauty in the southern limestone region of the Peak District. A gem of a caravan site nestled in the grounds of Ilam Park with stunning views towards Dovedale)

Upper Booth Farm
Edale
Hope Valley
Derbyshire S33 7ZJ
OS Grid Ref: SK103854
Tel: 01433 670250
Email: mail@helliwell.info
www.upperboothcamping.co.uk
(Situated on a working hill-farm on the High Peak Estate in the Peak District National Park)

Houghton Mill
Mill Street
Houghton
Nr Huntingdon
Cambridgeshire PE28 2AZ
OS Grid Ref: 153:TL283720
Tel: 01480 466716
www.caravanclub.co.uk
(A delightful site on the banks of the River Ouse overlooking Houghton Mill, on the edge of the picturesque village of Houghton. Easily accessible from A14, A1 and M11. Milling demonstrations are held every Sunday during the season. The area is a paradise for walkers and bird-watchers)

Penlan Caravan Park
Penlan
Brilley
Nr Hay on Wye
Herefordshire HR3 6JW
OS Grid Ref: 148:SO280515
Tel: 01497 831485
*(Small, peaceful, secluded site offering
magnificent southern views)*

NORTH EAST

Cut Thorn Farm
Gibside
Burnopfield
Newcastle-upon-Tyne
Tyne & Wear NE16 6AA
OS Grid Ref: 88: NZ172583
Tel: 01207 270230
*(With views across the Derwent Valley,
the site is surrounded by woodland)*

Haltwhistle
The Holiday Manager
Camping and Caravanning Club Site
Burnfoot Park Village
Haltwhistle
Northumberland NE49 0JP
OS Grid Ref: 87:NY685621
Tel: 01434 320106 (not after 8pm)
www.campingandcaravanning
   club.co.uk
*(A pretty campsite alongside a river
which is ideal for fishing. Close to
Hadrian's Wall and the Pennine Way)*

Nostell Priory Holiday Park
Doncaster Road
Nostell
Wakefield
West Yorkshire WF4 1QE
OS Grid Ref: 111:SE407173
Tel: 01924 863938 or 01924 864045
Email: reception@nostellpriory
   holidaypark.co.uk
www.nostellprioryholidaypark.co.uk
*(Picturesque and tranquil woodland
holiday park, with small shop and play
area. Pitches for touring caravans,
motorhomes and tents. Limited number
of privately owned caravan holiday
homes available for rent)*

NORTH WEST

Dodgson Wood Campsite
Nibthwaite Grange Farm
Nr Ulverston
Cumbria LA12 8DB
OS Grid Ref: SD301924
Tel: 01229 885663 or 07767 272970
*(An ideal base for walking, mountain
biking or water activities)*

Great Langdale
Manager
Great Langdale Camp Site
Great Langdale
Nr Ambleside
Cumbria LA22 9JU
OS Grid Ref: 89:NY287058
Tel: 01539 463862
Email: langdale.camp@national
    trust.org.uk
www.ntlakescampsites.org.uk
*(An excellent base for fell walking
and rock climbing)*

Low Manesty Caravan Club Site
Manesty Keswick
Cumbria CA12 5UG
OS Grid Ref: 90:NY251187
Tel: 01768 777275
www.caravanclub.co.uk
*(Set in woodland close to Derwentwater
with wide diversity of wildlife)*

Low Park Wood Caravan Club Site
The Warden
Sedgwick
Kendal
Cumbria LA8 0JZ 7
OS Grid Ref: 97:SD509878
Tel: 01539 560186 or 01539 561869
www.caravanclub.co.uk
*(Peaceful riverside site close to a river,
providing wonderful opportunities for
bird-watching and fishing)*

Low Wray
Campsite Manager
Low Wray National Trust Camp Site
Ambleside
Cumbria LA22 OJA7
OS Grid Ref: 96 & 97:NY372012
Tel: 015394 63862
www.ntlakescampsites.org.uk
*(Situated on the western shore of Lake
Windermere. Excellent base for walking,
sailing, canoeing and windsurfing)*

Park Coppice Caravan Club Site
The Warden
Coniston
Cumbria LA21 8LA
OS Grid Ref: 96:SD297957
Tel: 01539 441555
www.caravanclub.co.uk
*(An imaginatively landscaped site in
woodland near Coniston Water)*

Seatoller Farm Camp Site
Borrowdale
Keswick
Cumbria CA12 5XN
OS Grid Ref: NY245135
Tel: 01768 777232
Email: info@seatoilerfarm.co.uk
www.seatollerfarm.co.uk
(Situated in a beautiful valley at the foot of the Honister Pass. Close to the Coast-to-Coast route and Scafell Pike)

Side Farm
Patterdale
Penrith
Cumbria CA11 0NP 7
OS Grid Ref: 90: NY386167
Tel: 01768 482337 or 07796 128897
www.lakedistrictcamping.co.uk/
    campsites/northeast/side_farm
(Quiet site beside Ullswater, an ideal base for walking, mountain biking, fishing, water activities or simply relaxing)

Wasdale Head
Wasdale National Trust Camp Site
Seascale
Cumbria CA20 1EX
OS Grid Ref: 89:NY183076
Tel: 01539 463862
www.ntlakescampsites.org.uk
(An excellent base for fell walking and rock climbing)

Tatton Park
Knutsford
Cheshire WA16 6QN
OS Grid Ref: 109 & 118:SS737815
Tel: 01625 534400 or 01625 534403
Email: tatton@cheshire.gov.uk
www.tattonpark.org.uk
(Tatton Park is one of England's finest estates. A Neo-classical mansion, 20.2 hectares (50 acres) of Tudor gardens, Tudor Old Hall working farm, all set in 405 hectares (1,000 acres) of magnificent parkland)

Wrostlers Barn Bothy
Nibthwaite
Grange Farm
Nr Ulverston
Cumbria LA12 8DB
OS Grid Ref: SD300926
Tel: 01229 885663 or 07767 272970
www.groupaccommodation.com
(Converted field barn in spectacular secluded position on the shores of Coniston Water. Converted from an isolated field barn, it is on the fringe of the Dodgson Wood, a Site of Special Scientific Interest)

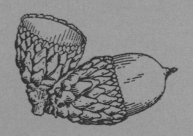

WALES

Carnedd
Gwern Gof Uchaf
Capel Curig
Betws-y-Coed
Conwy LL24 0EU
OS Grid Ref: 115:SH673604
Tel: 01690 720294
www.tryfanwales.co.uk
*(Site on traditional hill-farm at
foot of Tryfan and Tryfan Bach,
ideally located for climbing and walking.
National Mountaineering Centre at
Plas-y-Brenin, offers courses in canoeing,
climbing and dry ski-slope skiing)*

Cwmrath Farm
Stepaside
Narberth
Pembrokeshire SA67 8LU
OS Grid Ref: 158:SN151077
Tel: 01834 812010
Email: info@pembrokeshirecoast
    organicmeat.co.uk
www.pembrokeshirecoastorganic
    meat.co.uk
*(Lawned 5.6 hectare (14 acre) site
on a friendly family organic farm near
Tenby, close to sandy Wiseman's Bridge
beach, Amroth)*

Dinas Island Farm
Dinas
Newport
Pembrokeshire SA42 0SE
OS Grid Ref: 157:SN010404
Tel: 01239 820208 or 07970 108390
*(Peaceful, unique coastal site enjoying
stunning views. Easy access to
Pembrokeshire Coast Path. Beach
at end of drive. Ideal family site)*

Gwern Gof Isaf Farm
Capel Curig Betws-y-Coed
Conwy LL24 0EU
OS Grid Ref: 115:SH686602
Tel: 01690 720276
www.gwerngofisaf.co.uk
*(Licensed campsite on 304 hectare
(751-acre) farm. Climbing and
abseiling on site. Cliffs nearby for
climbing or walking. National
Mountaineering Centre at
Plas-y-Brenin, offers courses
in canoeing, climbing and dry
ski-slope skiing)*

Hafod y Llan
Craflwyn
Beddgelert
Gwynedd LL55 4NG
OS Grid Ref: 115:SH620510
Tel: 01766 510129 or 01766 510145
www.nationaltrust.org.uk/main/
   w-vh/w-holidays/w-camp.htm
*(Farm is managed to enhance the
landscape, nature conservation and its
amenity value while ensuring economic
benefit to the community through
traditional farming. The site is adjacent
to the farm, next to a mountain stream
and is conveniently located for walks up
Snowdon and public transport)*

Lleithyr Meadow Caravan Club Site
The Warden
Whitesands
St David's
Pembrokeshire SA62 6PR
OS Grid Ref: 145:SM746271
Tel: 01437 720401
www.caravanclub.co.uk
*(An open site close to three headlands on
the lovely Pembrokeshire coast, so ideal for
swimming, surfing, windsurfing and
sailing. Nearby bird sanctuaries on
offshore islands make it a birder's
paradise. Day trips to some of them from
Martin's Haven, about 20miles (32km)
along the coast)*

Ogofau Caravan Site
Dolaucothi Gold Mines
Pumsaint
Llanwrda
Carmarthenshire SA19 8US
OS Grid Ref: 146:SN668405
Tel: 01558 650365/650809
Email: dolaucothi@national
   trust.org.uk
www.nationaltrust.org.uk
*(Attractive twin-level site in woodland
glade within 90m (100yd) of the River
Cothi. Abundance of wild flowers and
birds, including rare Red Kite. Fishing
on the River Cothi with winter storage.
Some hardstanding)*

Penbryn Beach
Llanborth Farm
Penbryn
Sarnau Llandyssul
Ceredigion SA44 6QL
OS Grid Ref: 145:SN295521
Tel: 01239 810389 or 07802 596936
*(Located on a working dairy farm at the
access to Penbryn Beach in the Hoffhant
Valley, on the Heritage Coast Path.
Coastal and woodland walks. Well
positioned for exploring the area)*

Pwll-caerog Farm
Berea
St David's
Haverfordwest
Pembrokeshire SA62 6DG
OS Grid Ref: 157:SN786302
Tel: 01348 837405
www.celtic-camping.co.uk
*(Small, friendly campsite on a working
Pembrokeshire farm. The site is 460m
(500yd) from the Pembrokeshire Coast
Path with spectacular views of Abereiddy
and Strumble Head. Ideal base for
walkers, divers, birdwatchers,
water-sports enthusiasts, outdoor
|pursuits groups and for enjoying the
beauties of the Pembrokeshire countryside)*

Rynys Farm Camping Site
Nr Betws-y-Coed
Llanrwst
Conwy LL26 0RU
OS Grid Ref: 115 & 116:SH815535
Tel: 01690 710218
www.rynys-camping.co.uk
*(Very scenic, peaceful site with excellent,
clean facilities and silence after 11pm)*

NORTHERN IRELAND

Castle Ward
Strangford Downpatrick
Co. Down BT30 7LS
OS Grid Ref: J5850
Tel: 02844 881204
Email: jacqueline.baird@national
   trust.org.uk
*(With views over Strangford Loch and
all its activities, the campsite is part of the
820 acre Castle Ward Estate, close to
plenty of woodland and garden walks)*

Springhill
Moneymore
Magherafelt
Co. Londonderry BT45 7NQ
OS Grid Ref: H866828
Tel: 028867 48210
Email: springhill@nationaltrust.org.uk
*(Close to Springhill House and ideal for
walks on the 10 acre estate. Close to the
quaint and tranquil village of
Moneymore)*

USEFUL ORGANISATIONS

Backpackers Club
Email: inforequest@backpackers
   club.co.uk
www.backpackersclub.co.uk

British Canoe Union
18 Market Place
Bingham
Nottingham NG13 8AP
Tel: 0845 370 9500 or 0300 0119 500
Email: info@bcu.org.uk
www.bcu.org.uk

Camping and Caravanning Club
Greenfields House
Westwood Way
Coventry CV4 8JH
Tel: 0845 130 7631 or 02476 475448
Email: via online form
www.campingandcaravanning
   club.co.uk

Canoe-Camping Club
(an active section of the Camping and
Caravanning Club)
Greenfields House
Westwood Way
Coventry CV4 8JH
Tel: 02476 475448
www.canoecampingclub.co.uk

Caravan Club
East Grinstead House
East Grinstead
West Sussex RH19 1UA
Tel: 01342 326 944
Email: enquiries@caravanclub.co.uk
www.caravanclub.co.uk

Cyclists' Touring Club
Parklands
Railton Rd
Guildford
Surrey GU2 9JX
Tel : 0844 736 8450
Email: cycling@ctc.org.uk
www.ctc.org.uk

Hill Walking Organization UK
www.hillwalking.org.uk

International Camping Club UK
www.internationalcampingclub.com

Mountain Biking UK
10 Waterside Way
Northampton NN4 7XD
Tel: 0844 848 2852
www.magazine.bikerider.com/category
  /mountain-biking-uk/

Ramblers Association
2nd Floor Camelford House
87–90 Albert Embankment
London SE1 7TW
Tel: 020 7339 8500
Email: ramblers@ramblers.org.uk
www.ramblers.org.uk

RSPB (Royal Society for the
Protection of Birds)
Contact via the online form
www.rspb.org.uk

CPRE (Campaign to Protect Rural
England)
128 Southwark Street
London, SE1 0SW
Tel: 020 7981 2800
Email: info@cpre.org.uk
www.cpre.org.uk

National Trust
PO Box 39
Warrington
WA5 7WD
Tel: 0844 800 1895
Email: enquiries@nationaltrust.org.uk
www.nationaltrust.org.uk

FURTHER READING

RSPB Pocket Nature: Wildlife of Britain (Dorling Kindersley, 2009)
Collins Nature Guide: Mushrooms and Toadstools of Britain and Europe by Brian
   Spooner (Collins, 1994)
Collins Nature Guide: Wild Animals of Britain and Europe by Helga Hoffman
   (Collins, 1995)
Sleeping in a Sack: Camping Activities for Kids by Linda White and Fran Lee
   (Gibbs M. Smith Inc, 1998)
Wild Food by Jane Eastoe (National Trust Books, 2008)
Hedgerow and Wildlife by Jane Eastoe (National Trust Books, 2008)
Book of the Countryside (National Trust Books, 2009)
Britain By Bike by Jane Eastoe (Batsford, 2010)

PICTURE CREDITS

© Bridgeman Art Library / page 2: Front cover of 'John Bull', February 1956 (colour litho) by English School, (20th century). Private Collection/ © The Advertising Archives/ The Bridgeman Art Library.

© FLPA / page 9 © Mark Sisson; page 51 top © Sandra Schanzer/Imagebroker; page 56 © Stefan Huwiler/Imagebroker; page 83 © Phil McLean; 145 bottom © Fritz Polking; page 148 © Adri Hoogendijk/Minden; page 149 © Herbert Kehrer/Imagebroker; page 150 © Tony Wharton; page 152 top © Malcolm Schuyl; page 162 © Cyril Ruoso/Minden; page 164 © Paul Hobson; page 165 © Erica Olsen; page 175 © Paul Hobson; page 176 and page 163 © Sean Hunter; page 179 © Robin Chittenden; page 180 © Cisca Castelijns/Minden; page 183 © Michael Krabs/Imagebroker; page 184 top © Andrew Bailey

© Mary Evans Picture Library / page 7; page 14; page 50; page 52; page 74; page 78; page 93; page 97; page 117; page 134; page 141; page 155; page 169; page 172; page 178; page 188; page 10, 35, 43, 103, 174 and 177 © Lucinda Gosling Collection/Mary Evans; page 11 © John Maclellan Collection/Mary Evans; page 24 and 122 © Grenville Collins Postcard Collection/Mary Evans; page 26 © IMAGNO/Austrian Archives (S)/Mary Evans; page 61 © courtesy of the estate of Mrs J.C.Robinson/Pollinger Ltd/Lucinda Gosling/Mary Evans; page 77 © Onslow Auctions Ltd/Mary Evans; page 81 © Lesley Bradshaw Collection/Mary Evans; page 113 © courtesy of the estate of Mrs J.C.Robinson/Pollinger Ltd/Mary Evans; page 132 © Country Life/IPC Media Ltd/Mary Evans; page 136 © IMAGNO/Osterreiches Volkshochschularchiv/MaryEvans; page 161 © Tom Gillmor Collection/Mary Evans.

© NTPL / page 6, 12, 17, 21, 23, 27, 32, 44–45, 46–47, 57, 58, 63, 64, 151 and 182–183 © Joe Cornish; page 8, 152 bottom and 160 © Andrew Butler; page 18, 41, 54–55, 65, 66, 80, 131, 167, 170 bottom and 186–187 © John Millar; page 19, 51 bottom, 62, 70 bottom, 96, 99, 142 © Paul Harris; page 30 bottom © William Shaw; page 39 © Britainonview/Rod Edwards; page 40, 88, 89, 107, 109 © David Levenson; page 42 ©Simon Fraser; page 48 ©Nadia Mackenzie; page 49 © Robert Morris; page 53, 59, 143 and 146–147 © David Noton; page 82 © Jennie Woodcock; page 84 © Stephen Robson; page 85 and 118 ©NTPL/Andrew Montgomery; page 98 and page 145 top © Paul Wakefield; page 105 © Ian Shaw; page 115 © Val Corbett; page 127 © Myles New; page 135 © Ross Hoddinott; page 139 © Michael Caldwell; page 140 © NTPL; page 181 © Nick Daly; page 184 bottom © Ben Selway.

INDEX